Fresh Hope for Today

for Today

Devotions for Joy on the Journey

GRACE FOX

AspirePress

Fresh Hope for Today: Devotions for Joy on the Journey
Copyright © 2022 Grace Fox

Published by Aspire Press
An imprint of Tyndale House Ministries
Carol Stream, Illinois
www.hendricksonrose.com

ISBN: 978-1-64938-055-5

The views and opinions expressed in this book are those of the author(s) and do not necessarily express the views of Tyndale House Ministries or Aspire Press, nor is this book intended to be a substitute for mental health treatment or professional counseling. The information in this resource is intended as guidelines for healthy living. Please consult qualified medical, legal, pastoral, and psychological professionals regarding individual concerns.

Scripture quotations, unless otherwise indicated, are taken from the Holy Bible, New International Version®, NIV®. Copyright © 1973, 1978, 1984, 2011 by Biblica, Inc.™ Used by permission of Zondervan. All rights reserved worldwide. www.zondervan.com The "NIV" and "New International Version" are trademarks registered in the United States Patent and Trademark Office by Biblica, Inc.™

Scripture quotations marked NLT are taken from the *Holy Bible*, New Living Translation®, Copyright © 1996, 2004, 2015 by Tyndale House Foundation. Used by permission of Tyndale House Publishers, Carol Stream, Illinois 60188. All rights reserved.

Scripture quotations marked NASB are taken from the New American Standard Bible® (NASB), Copyright © 1960, 1971, 1977, 1995, 2020 by The Lockman Foundation. Used by permission. All rights reserved. www.lockman.org

Scripture quotations are from the ESV® Bible (The Holy Bible, English Standard Version®), copyright © 2001 by Crossway, a publishing ministry of Good News Publishers. Used by permission. All rights reserved.

Book design by Cristalle Kishi

Printed in the United States of America
010422VP

This book is given to

_____

on this day

_____

Contents

Dear Friend,

Welcome aboard, fellow traveler. I'm so glad we can take this faith journey together. It's comforting to have a companion when the road on which we walk feels lonely or steep. It's reassuring to hear the stories of others who have gone before us and know the way. And it's encouraging to discover, or be reminded of, truths from God's Word that shed light on our path, especially when it takes an unexpected detour.

No matter where our journey leads, we can know for certain that God goes with us and cares for us. We can face the road ahead with hope for a good outcome under his sovereignty. His promises to guard, guide, and give us every reason to choose and experience joy. My prayer is that the words on each page will restore your hope and renew your joy—and do so abundantly.

Dear God, thank you for providing travel companions for this journey called life. Please lead my friend along the path you've chosen. Grant strength when the way feels wearisome and peace when it perplexes. Give hope on dark days. Grant joy in sunshine and in shadow. I pray this in the power of your name with thanks in advance. Amen.

Know you are loved,

Grace Fox

God Is in the Details

The LORD directs the steps of the godly.
He delights in every detail of their lives.

PSALM 37:23 NLT

Pause

My husband (whom I've nicknamed Sailor-Man) and I left our marina, intending to spend a week-long working vacation on our boat-home before returning to help our son with a project. Our calendar cleared when our son canceled his plans.

Rather than return to our marina, we decided to combine working from the boat with traveling to the area where we used to live, while stopping to visit friends in a few coastal communities along the way.

One get-together was especially meaningful. We'd known Tom and Linda for twenty-five years and shared a lot of history. We recalled fun memories and swapped current stories for an hour. Fellowship was sweet, and goodbyes came too soon.

Tom passed away nine days later. The news shocked us, but it didn't surprise God. He knew what was coming. I believe he gave us the idea to take a working vacation so that we'd continue traveling up the coast when our son canceled his plans. One decision led to another, so we could visit Tom once more before he moved to heaven. God was in every detail.

Ponder

How have you seen God in the details when your plans changed unexpectedly?

Pray

God, take my journey in the direction you want, so your purposes can be accomplished.

"Who is God? He is the Lord. He is the Sovereign Ruler of the universe. He knows what you're feeling and why. He knows what you need, and he will give it as you can receive it. He is a rock—strong, bold, mighty, immovable, unyielding in power. The Lord your God will guide you right."

PETER M. WALLACE

Joy Defined

Always be joyful. Never stop praying.
Be thankful in all circumstances, for this is
God's will for you who belong to Christ Jesus.

1 THESSALONIANS 5:16–18 NLT

Pause

God commands us to always be joyful. We can easily obey that command when everything's going well, but how can we do it when our journey leads through disappointments and dark valleys? Here's where it's helpful to understand what joy is.

My favorite definition, which was coined by Kay Warren in *Choose Joy: Because Happiness Isn't Enough*, is "Joy is the settled assurance that God is in control of all the details of my life, the quiet confidence that ultimately everything is going to be all right, and the determined choice to praise God in every situation."

Joy isn't a fleeting feeling based on happy circumstances. It's an unshakable emotion that says everything's going to be okay because God is wise, loving, good, and sovereign, and he still sits on the throne. It takes root and grows deep when we choose to praise God, even when things aren't going well, and it enables us to hold on to hope for a good outcome.

God never issues an impossible command. Joy at all times, good and bad, is his desire for us, and it becomes our reality when we trust him unconditionally.

Ponder

What's your definition of joy?

Pray

God, thank you for making lasting joy a possibility, because you are who you say you are.

"Christian joy is a good feeling in the soul, produced by the Holy Spirit, as he causes us to see the beauty of Christ in the word and in the world."

JOHN PIPER, author of *Desiring God*

The Spirit's Fruit

The Holy Spirit produces this kind of fruit
in our lives: love, joy, peace, patience,
kindness, goodness, faithfulness,
gentleness, and self-control.

GALATIANS 5:22–23 NLT

Pause

My oldest daughter and her husband live in an arid region of Washington state. The road between their home and our marina winds through hills that resemble the set for a western movie, complete with sagebrush and rattlesnakes.

Interestingly, some of those same hills are able to sustain orchards of apples, peaches, pears, and grapes. We can spot the orchards from miles away because irrigation turns them a lush green—a stark contrast to the sunbaked brown around them.

As Christ's followers, we ought to stand in stark contrast to the world around us—especially when facing hardship. Our ability to experience joy despite heartache and tears bears witness to God's presence and supernatural work within us.

Joy is not the typical response to trouble, nor is it something we can produce on our own. The Holy Spirit produces it in direct proportion to the access we give him to our lives. The more authority we allow him, the more spiritual fruit he grows in us, even when difficulties surround us.

Ponder

Do others see joy produced in your life?

Pray

God, make my life like a lush orchard that produces joy as a fruit of your Holy Spirit.

"Hope fills the afflicted soul with such inward joy and consolation, that it can laugh while tears are in the eye, sigh and sing all in a breath; it is called 'the rejoicing of hope' (Hebrews 3:6)."

WILLIAM GURNALL,
The Christian in Complete Armour;
or a Treatise on the Saints' War with the Devil

The Rain Will Stop

*Then they cried to the LORD in their trouble,
and he delivered them from their distress.*

PSALM 107:28 ESV

Pause

Sailor-Man and I woke to the sound of rain pelting our boat. We were anchored far from shore, and the nearest town was at least two hours away—too far to motor across sloppy seas for no other reason than to escape our confined space. Riding out the storm was our only option, so we hunkered down inside and hoped the weather would clear.

Morning rolled into afternoon. A couple more hours passed and then, finally, the sunshine poked through the clouds. Its warmth wooed us, grateful, from our mini-ark.

Life's storms come and go like rainstorms. When they're present, they might feel as though they're here to stay. But this we know: the clouds *will* part and the sun *will* shine in God's good time. He's working in ways we can neither see nor understand, and he will deliver us from our distress when he has fulfilled his purposes.

Be patient. Hang on to hope as you hunker down. He hears your cries for help, and he will bring this rainy day—or season—to an end at the proper time.

Ponder

What's your attitude as you wait for the rain to stop?

Pray

God, teach me to hunker down with a hope-filled heart until the rain stops.

"He knows when we go into the storm,
He watches over us in the storm,
and He can bring us out of the storm
when His purposes have been fulfilled."

WARREN W. WIERSBE,
Looking Up When Life Gets You Down

Good Trumps Evil

Pause

The pandemic forced us down roads we never thought we'd travel, and the journey has been painful. In the midst of hardship, however, we can wake to fresh hope every morning, because God is sovereign over our circumstances. Nothing bad happens to us that he cannot turn into something good. We can face our challenges with confidence because he has proven this is true.

In the Bible, the ultimate tragedy took place when Jesus, the sinless son of God, suffered and died by crucifixion on a wooden cross. The sky turned black, the earth shook, and evil claimed victory when Jesus breathed his last. But God's best work had only begun. Three days later, Jesus rose from the dead. He conquered the power of evil and death for all who place their faith in him for salvation.

What Satan means for evil, God intends for good. We might not see good trump evil as quickly as we might wish, but it will happen. Hold on to hope. God isn't finished yet.

Ponder

How have you seen God trump evil with good in your life?

Pray

God, your ultimate tragedy gives me ultimate victory. I am eternally grateful.

> "The cross stands as the final symbol that no evil exists that God cannot turn into a blessing. He is the living Alchemist who can take the dregs from the slag-heaps of life—disappointment, frustration, sorrow, disease, death, economic loss, heartache— and transform the dregs into gold."
>
> CATHERINE MARSHALL,
> *Beyond Our Selves*

Loved

God showed his great love for us by sending
Christ to die for us while we were still sinners.

ROMANS 5:8 NLT

Pause

Denyse had experienced a lot of pain in her life. Poor personal choices heaped heartache on her, and others' choices added more. Her siblings labeled her a drama queen, and coworkers excluded her from lunchroom conversations. Hers was a lonely existence, and she felt she deserved it.

Denyse could scarcely believe it when a friend told her that Jesus loved her. She'd always assumed he wouldn't want to associate with someone who didn't have her act together, so she'd never explored teachings about him. Learning that he came to earth to bring hope and to help her flourish changed her mind (John 3:17).

Jesus loves us because of who he is—the sinless son of God who came to earth for sinners' sake. He never rejects us because we carry hurts. In fact, he does the opposite: he invites us to bring him our doubts, failures, disappointments, and imperfections, so he can heal us. He doesn't expect us to have our act together before he accepts us. He accepts us, and then he helps us get our act together.

Ponder

What hurts would you like to bring to Jesus?

Pray

God, I come to you just as I am. Thank you for loving me in this state.

> "If we comprehend what Christ has done for us, then surely out of gratitude we will strive to live 'worthy' of such great love. We will strive for holiness not to make God love us but because God already does."
>
> PHILIP YANCEY,
> *Grace Notes: Daily Readings with a Fellow Pilgrim*

Celebrate

We had to celebrate this happy day.
For your brother was dead
and has come back to life!
He was lost, but now he is found!

LUKE 15:32 NLT

Pause

The story of the prodigal son paints an amazing word picture of God's desire for relationship with us. Imagine the prodigal's father scanning the horizon every day, waiting for his son's return. His wait is finally rewarded.

The father runs down the road, throwing dignity to the wind. He hugs and kisses his boy. He interrupts an apology with calls for the servants to fetch the finest robe, some sandals, and a ring. And then he says, "Let's party!"

My friend, this is the Father's affection for us. This is his joy over us. Sometimes we doubt his forgiveness and acceptance. We mess up and then feel unworthy to be with him. We pull away and hide from him, assuming he'll punish us and ban us from his presence. Nothing's further from the truth.

Our heavenly Father longs for our return, so let's not keep him waiting. When we sin, let's confess and receive his forgiveness (1 John 1:9). Restored relationship restores joy—both ours and his—and deserves celebration.

Ponder

How do you think the heavenly Father views you?

Pray

God, keep me mindful that our relationship brings you joy. Help me view it as something to celebrate.

> "Our Lord loves us so much that He is more than willing to forgive us and throw a 'feast' for us when we repent and ask for his forgiveness."
>
> PATRICK BALDWIN,
> *Reflections of Faith: Learn about Prayer, Purity, Hope, and Faith to Live a Full Christian Life with the Blessings of God*

Good from Pain

[God's] anger lasts only a moment, but his favor lasts a lifetime! Weeping may last through the night, but joy comes with the morning.

PSALM 30:5 NLT

Pause

The story is told of a man who noticed a butterfly struggling to emerge from a teeny hole in its silky cocoon. It wriggled and wrestled but to no avail. Assuming the butterfly was stuck, the man gently widened the hole. Then he watched and waited. Imagine his disappointment when the butterfly finally appeared with shriveled wings and a swollen body.

Unaware that the wriggling and wrestling were part of the butterfly's natural process to prepare for flight, the man sought to spare the butterfly discomfort, but his actions disrupted the natural process and destroyed the butterfly's ability to fly.

No one likes to endure pain or watch someone else experience it. We'd rather avoid it, but that's not necessarily best for us. If we allow it, pain can teach us patience and perseverance, make us aware of our weaknesses, and lead us to a deeper dependence on God's strength. It teaches us to rely on his promises and be more attuned to his presence.

God always has a purpose for our pain, and it is good because he is good.

Ponder

What good things have come from your pain?

Pray

God, I trust you to bring good from pain because you are good.

> "The marvelous richness of human experience would lose something of rewarding joy if there were no limitations to overcome. The hilltop hour would not be half so wonderful if there were no dark valleys to traverse."
>
> HELEN KELLER, *The Open Door*

God-Sized Assignments

*May [God] equip you with all you need
for doing his will. May he produce in you,
through the power of Jesus Christ, every
good thing that is pleasing to him.*

HEBREWS 13:21 NLT

Pause

At the time my first book launched, my family lived in an island community with one gas station, a couple of small grocery stores, and no traffic lights. Imagine my panic, then, when my publisher arranged a media tour and made me responsible to drive myself from studio to studio.

I flew to Chicago to begin the tour. When a car rental agency clerk handed me a set of keys, I said, "The next time you see my face might be on a missing person poster." He laughed. I didn't. Before leaving my parking stall, I patted the front passenger seat and prayed, "Jesus, it's me and you. I can't do this without your help."

Our faith journey often includes God-sized assignments that leave us feeling scared and inadequate, like Moses felt when God told him to lead the Israelites from Egypt. I'm so thankful that God always equips us for our tasks. He never expects us to do them on our own.

Ponder

What God-sized task has God given you?

Pray

God, I'm willing to do whatever you ask because you don't expect me to do it in my own strength.

> "I discovered an astonishing truth: God is attracted to weakness. He can't resist those who humbly and honestly admit how desperately they need him. Our weakness, in fact, makes room for his power."
>
> JIM CYMBALA,
> *Fresh Wind, Fresh Fire: What Happens When God's Spirit Invades the Heart of His People*

Rescue

The LORD says, "I will rescue those
who love me. I will protect those
who trust in my name."

PSALM 91:14 NLT

Pause

My second media tour began in Florida. After my interview there, a friend drove me to the airport for my flight to Chicago. It was a balmy January day, so I'd tossed my coat on the backseat of her car. Unfortunately, I forgot it there.

Chicago greeted me with a blizzard. My connecting flight was canceled, so I rode a bus to my next destination. By the time I arrived, the rental agency where I'd reserved a car had already closed. There I stood in a strange city at midnight, in a blizzard, without a coat. "God, rescue me!" I prayed.

Moments later, a woman approached and asked if I needed help. I explained my situation and she said, "My husband is an off-duty taxi driver. He'll take you to your hotel." The same man returned the next morning—with a coat in hand—and drove me to and from my interview.

I've often wondered whether the man was an angel in disguise. Maybe he was. Maybe not. Regardless, the Lord kept his promise to rescue me, and I will always be grateful.

Ponder

From what do you need God to rescue you?

Pray

God, I need your help. I trust in your name and in your faithfulness to keep your promise to rescue me.

"Do you need help today? Lift up your hands to the Lord in supplication and in expectation, and soon you will lift up your hands in jubilation and celebration."

WARREN W. WIERSBE,
Prayer, Praise and Promises: A Daily Walk through the Psalms

Use Your Gifts

*God has given each of you a gift from
his great variety of spiritual gifts.
Use them well to serve one another.*

1 PETER 4:10 NLT

Pause

God designed each of us as one-of-a-kind, and we each play a unique role in his kingdom. He has given us talents and spiritual gifts to fulfill our role (Romans 12:3–8; 1 Corinthians12:8–10, 28). Using those gifts brings joy to others and bounces back to bless us.

Unfortunately, we sometimes fail to use or appreciate our God-given gifts. Perhaps we don't know how to identify them. Maybe fear of failure restrains us from exploring or using them. Sometimes circumstances beyond our control—or our present season of life—prevent us from putting them to work.

The comparison trap is another hindrance. We either presume that our gifts are more important than others and grow proud, or we assume they're lesser than that of others and grow fearful of rejection.

Jesus came to earth to serve, and we're to follow in his footsteps. We don't have to be super-accomplished or aaah-mazing to be a blessing in God's kingdom. We only need to be willing to say yes to opportunities where our unique design can make a difference.

Ponder

What are your God-given gifts, talents, and passions?

Pray

God, open my eyes to see opportunities to use my unique design to serve.

> "You have inside you the capacity to invest
> your mental, emotional, and spiritual gifts
> in a way that glorifies God, impacts the world,
> and satisfies your own soul. I believe that—
> and I want you to believe it, too."
>
> DAVID JEREMIAH

Equipped

We are God's masterpiece. He has created
us anew in Christ Jesus, so we can do the
good things he planned for us long ago.

EPHESIANS 2:10 NLT

Pause

At some point along our life's journey, God will ask us to do something far beyond our human capability. In their book *Experiencing God: Knowing and Doing the Will of God*, Henry and Richard Blackaby say that our response to God's call reveals what we believe to be true about God and that this is a "crisis of belief."

Moses experienced such a crisis when God appointed him to lead the Israelites' exodus from Egypt. He immediately focused on his inadequacies rather than on God's presence and promises to help him, and he questioned God's wisdom in choosing him for the task (Exodus 3:11).

Remembering that God always equips us to fulfill a divine assignment prevents us from falling into the same mistaken beliefs. We can say yes, knowing the God never tells us to do something that is impossible in the strength he provides.

Moses eventually did say yes. As a result, he witnessed God do miracles and experienced his character in ways that wouldn't have happened otherwise.

Saying yes when we're scared isn't comfortable, but it's the stepping-stone to experiencing God's power in ways we don't want to miss.

Ponder

Recall a crisis of belief, or faith, you've experienced. How did you respond?

Pray

God, help me say yes, even if it means saying it scared.

"Our God is the God of the impossible. When we say yes to doing new things as we step into our destiny, we'll get to see God show up and equip us for the journey ahead in miraculous ways."

CHRISTINE CAINE

Five Loaves, Two Fish

Here is a boy with five small barley
loaves and two small fish, but how
far will they go among so many?

JOHN 6:9

Pause

I was a stay-at-home mom when I ventured into writing for publication. I did so only because I felt God calling me to the task. With no formal training and no knowledge about the publishing industry, I attended a writers' conference to learn.

The fear of inadequacy and failure followed me there and home, but I feared the consequences of disobeying God more, so I prayed daily, "Father, I'm the child with five loaves and two fish. I offer you my meager skills and knowledge about writing. Take them and make a miracle."

I had no clue how God could or would use my offering. That was up to him. My responsibility was to make myself available and follow his lead.

My friend, God has designed and gifted you in unique ways for his glory. Don't let fear stop you from obeying his call. Share with him what he's given you just as the boy shared his loaves and fish. You might feel as though you have little to offer, but little is much in God's hands.

Ponder

What resource, skill, or talent can you offer to Jesus?

Pray

God, here's my meager offering. Take it and make a kingdom miracle.

> "This journey is a chance to lay out what you have, what you know, and hand it up to God. I should mention: we have no idea what he will say to do with it, but we begin by laying it out and handing it over."
>
> JENNIE ALLEN,
> *Restless: Because You Were Made for More*

Not Alone

Don't be afraid, for I am with you.
Don't be discouraged, for I am your God.
I will strengthen you and help you.
I will hold you up with my victorious right hand.

ISAIAH 41:10 NLT

Pause

I'd traveled to Poland on my own to speak at a women's retreat, and Sailor-Man was scheduled to join me a week later. There was only one problem: I would have to take an eight-hour train ride to meet him. The thought rattled me for two reasons: (1) I don't speak or understand Polish, and (2) I am directionally challenged. My imagination said that I'd miss my connections or catch the wrong train. So did my mother. "I wish you didn't have to travel alone," she said.

Mom's words gave me a spiritual aha moment. I would be alone—but not really. God promises his presence everywhere and at all times; therefore, he would be my companion and help me find my way. I held on to his promise, and he kept his word.

As you face the road before you, know you are not alone. God is with you and will help you. Hold on to his promise, and he will keep his word.

Ponder

What lies is your imagination telling you about the road you're traveling?

Pray

God, guard my mind from fear by reminding me that you are with me and will help me.

> "Mostly I think I've learned to trust God more. I mean, if I start getting worried or freaked, I just try to put it in God's hands. Sometimes I imagine God cradling the globe in his hands, and I tell myself that as long as I'm with God, the Creator of the universe, I can be comfortable and at home anyplace on the planet."
>
> MELODY CARLSON,
> *Notes from a Spinning Planet—Mexico*

Don't Look Back

Brothers, I do not consider that I have made
it my own. But one thing I do: forgetting what
lies behind and straining forward to what
lies ahead, I press on toward the goal
for the prize of the upward call of
God in Christ Jesus.

PHILIPPIANS 3:13–14 ESV

Pause

Lot's family lived in the infamous city of Sodom. One day, angels warned Lot of God's coming judgment on the city's inhabitants and urged him to leave town. Lot hesitated, so the angels grabbed him and his family, pulled them to the city's outskirts, and told them to run far and fast without looking back. Sadly, Mrs. Lot stole a backward glance and became a pillar of salt (Genesis 19:15–26).

We might think God's response was a bit harsh, but it reveals truth that's vital to our faith journey. God wants us to make a complete break from sin, because he is holy and cannot associate with it. Further, entertaining desire for the things that grieve and offend him will lead us down the wrong path and destroy us.

The angels came to rescue Lot; Jesus came to rescue us. Run far and fast from sin, and refuse to look back.

Ponder

Are you casting a longing look at a particular sin? If so, name it.

Pray

God, rescue me from my desire to return to anything that grieves you and hurts me.

> "You cannot change the past, but the past can change you.... The past can be a rudder that guides you or an anchor that burdens you. Leave your past mistakes with God, and look to the future by faith."
>
> WARREN W. WIERSBE,
> *With the Word: The Chapter-by-Chapter Bible Handbook*

Forgiveness

*Be kind to each other, tenderhearted, forgiving one
another, just as God through Christ has forgiven you.*

EPHESIANS 4:32 NLT

Pause

Elyse wrestled with anger, grief, and disbelief for months
after her husband unexpectedly left their marriage. She
woke with headaches, and she lost both appetite and
motivation. Realizing she was standing on the brink of a
dark emotional abyss, she sought professional biblical
counseling. Part of that counseling involved a discussion
about forgiveness.

Elyse acknowledged the pain her husband's betrayal
caused, and she realized that, for her own well-being,
she needed to forgive him whether or not he asked for it.
Working through the process restored her physical, mental,
emotional, and spiritual health.

God created us and knows how we flourish best; therefore,
he commands us to forgive. Consider it like a doctor's order

for our spiritual well-being. Harboring resentment causes self-inflicted pain, but dealing with it appropriately brings healing to every part of who we are.

We can trust God to hold the offender accountable. At the same time, he holds us accountable for our response. So let's respond in a way that honors God and frees us to experience fresh hope and renewed joy on our journey.

Ponder

Do you need to forgive someone so that you can flourish again? If so, who?

Pray

God, grant me both the desire and the ability to forgive those who hurt me.

"In the shadow of my hurt, forgiveness feels like a decision to reward my enemy. But in the shadow of the cross, forgiveness is merely a gift from one undeserving soul to another."

ANDY STANLEY, *It Came from Within! The Shocking Truth of What Lurks in the Heart*

Joy Restored

Oh, what joy for those whose disobedience is forgiven,
whose sin is put out of sight! Yes, what joy for those
whose record the LORD has cleared of guilt,
whose lives are lived in complete honesty!

PSALM 32:1-2 NLT

Pause

We don't have to look deep into the lives of biblical heroes to know they weren't perfect: Noah got drunk. Moses killed a man. David committed adultery. Abraham lied to protect his hide. And the list goes on.

We dare not point our fingers too long, though, because we're not perfect, either. Every person on the planet fails. We all fall short of God's holy standard (Romans 3:23).

Those who have placed their faith in Jesus experience the Holy Spirit's conviction for sin. He doesn't condemn or shame us, but he puts his finger on a specific attitude or behavior that grieves God. Until we cooperate with him by confessing that sin, we find our joy in short supply.

Confessing our sin to Jesus helps restore our joy. He wipes our slate clean and gives us a fresh start. Forgiveness removes every reason to hide from him. With confidence, we can run to him, knowing he waits with open arms.

Ponder

How do you respond when the Holy Spirit convicts you of sin?

Pray

God, forgive my sin so that I might experience abundant joy in my relationship with you.

"Happiness is impossible without repentance, forgiveness, and a right relationship with Christ."

RANDY ALCORN,
God's Promise of Happiness

True Wealth

Our hearts ache, but we always have joy.
We are poor, but we give spiritual riches to others.
We own nothing, and yet we have everything.

2 CORINTHIANS 6:10 NLT

Pause

Sailor-Man and I sat on the floor with about two hundred Nepalese worshipers. Beside me sat a woman dressed in traditional village garb. The stubs that were once her fingers and toes evidenced leprosy.

Village women face limited opportunities, so I assumed she was illiterate. She proved me wrong when she opened her Bible. Its weathered pages and underlined verses told me she'd spent much time reading it. I watched as she moved one finger stub along the page, following the pastor's voice word by word as he read the day's passage. I felt both moved and convicted when my new friend positioned herself on her knees and bowed in reverence at the pastor's invitation to pray. I felt inspired as she mingled with others, smiling and praying with them after the service.

I couldn't understand much of the sermon, but God spoke volumes to me that day. His mouthpiece was a woman who'd obviously known heartache but who also knew Jesus. A woman who, though poor by the world's standards, owned a wealth of spiritual riches.

Ponder

Who do you know who demonstrates joy despite suffering?

Pray

God, grant me the ability to be joyful despite difficult circumstances.

"It is a remarkable thing that some of the most optimistic and enthusiastic people you will meet are those who have been through intense suffering."

WARREN W. WIERSBE,
Looking Up When Life Gets You Down

Wait

*I wait for the LORD, my whole being waits,
and in his word I put my hope. I wait for the
LORD more than watchmen wait for the morning,
more than watchmen wait for the morning.*

PSALM 130:5-6

Pause

We spend a significant part of our life's journey waiting for something to happen. We wait for a baby's birth, and then we can hardly wait until he or she walks. We wait for appointments, for a good sale, for a prodigal child's return, and for pandemics to end. As we wait, we hope for a good outcome.

The psalmist waited on the Lord to come to his rescue. Banking on God's promises, he hoped for a good outcome without losing faith. He compared himself to a night watchman scanning the horizon for the first glimmer of dawn. The watchman didn't know the exact moment it would appear, but he knew beyond a doubt that the light *would* crack the darkness. It was just a matter of time.

Waiting is not passive. Sometimes it takes our whole being to remain hopeful as we wait on the Lord to rescue us, but don't give up. He'll come. It's just a matter of time.

Ponder

What inspires you to remain hopeful when the wait seems long?

Pray

God, give me patience and confident hope like a night watchman waiting for dawn.

> "'Wait on the Lord' is a constant in the Psalms, and it is a necessary word, for God often keeps us waiting. He is not in such a hurry as we are, and it is not his way to give more light on the future than we need for action in the present, or to guide us more than one step at a time. When in doubt, do nothing, but continue to wait on God. When action is needed, light will come."
>
> J. I. PACKER, *Knowing God*

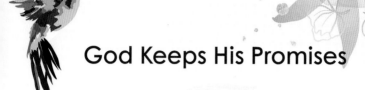

God Keeps His Promises

Say to them, "Thus says the LORD GOD:
None of my words will be delayed any longer,
but the word that I speak will be performed,
declares the LORD GOD."

EZEKIEL 12:28 ESV

Pause

My oldest daughter and I were separated when she was three days old. Born in Nepal with serious medical issues, she needed a life-saving procedure. My husband took her to the United States while I remained in Kathmandu. The international airline declared me a medical risk and said I must recover for a week before traveling.

With no guarantee that my baby would survive that long, saying goodbye was the most difficult thing I'd ever done. But God gave me hope by promising that his faithfulness would meet our family at every corner.

Counting on God's promise got me through the week. It gave me strength to get out of bed every morning, peace when I went to bed at night, and hope during the hours in between.

God cannot lie. When he makes a promise, he always keeps it. He will do what he says he will do. Standing on his promises ensures we're on firm footing. Our hope remains steadfast, even when extraordinary difficulty strikes.

Ponder

What promise has God made that fills you with hope today?

Pray

God, thank you for being completely reliable. Knowing you cannot lie gives me faith to trust you more.

> "We like to control the map of our life and know everything well in advance. But faith is content just knowing that God's promise cannot fail. This, in fact, is the excitement of walking with God."
>
> JIM CYMBALA, *Fresh Faith: What Happens When Real Faith Ignites God's People*

Love in Action

This is how God loved the world:
He gave his one and only Son,
so that everyone who believes in him
will not perish but have eternal life.

JOHN 3:16 NLT

Pause

A distant relative named Joanie lives in a hamlet in Manitoba, Canada. When the pandemic struck, she felt God nudge her to put love into action. She baked a loaf of bread, bagged it, and set it in a basket at the end of her driveway with a Free sign. One loaf led to another. Word of mouth spread, and "The Bread Basket" began drawing people from miles around. The price was right and the taste was even better, but I suspect the love baked into each loaf was the real magnet.

We live in a hurting world. Some folks are honest about their struggles, but many hide behind a plastic smile. Their facade masks their pain, but it can't ease or remove it. That's where love comes in.

We don't have to do great deeds to make a difference in someone's life. A little deed done with love works wonders. It instills hope by communicating to the recipient that she matters to us and to God.

Ponder

What's one kindness you can offer to someone who needs a little love today?

Pray

God, give me eyes to see those who are hurting and creative ideas for showing them your love.

"What does love look like? It has the hands to help others. It has the feet to hasten to the poor and needy. It has eyes to see misery and want. It has the ears to hear the sighs and sorrows of men. That is what love looks like."

AUGUSTINE OF HIPPO

Service

*Even the Son of Man came not to be served
but to serve others and to give his life
as a ransom for many.*

MARK 10:45 NLT

Pause

Given that Jesus was God's son, he could have expected others to serve him during his earthly journey. Consider his relationship with his disciples, for instance. Imagine the ease of doing life with a dozen personal assistants to fetch food and water, wash one's laundry, and mend one's sandals. But this was not Jesus' way.

Jesus poured his life into the disciples during his three-year ministry. Hours before he died, he stooped and washed their filthy feet—a task usually performed by the least important servants. Then he said, "I have given you an example to follow. Do as I have done to you" (John 13:15 NLT).

Our journey is not about us. We're here to serve others without hesitancy or complaint, even if it requires personal sacrifice. This is the pathway to the abundant life Jesus promises. It's also a path to joy, for as Jesus said, "I have told you these things so that you will be filled with my joy. Yes, your joy will overflow!" (John 15:11 NLT).

Ponder

How can you bless someone today through an act of service?

Pray

God, grant me a heart that loves to serve without hesitancy or complaint.

> "Serve the ones who hate you; forgive the ones who hurt you. Take the lowest place, not the highest; seek to serve, not to be served."
>
> MAX LUCADO,
> *Life Lessons from Ezra and Nehemiah: Lessons in Leadership*

Discipline

No discipline is enjoyable while it is happening—
it's painful! But afterward there will be
a peaceful harvest of right living for those
who are trained in this way.

HEBREWS 12:11 NLT

Pause

Everyone on a faith journey with Jesus will sooner or later experience God's discipline. Between you and me, my knee-jerk response to the word *discipline* is not warm and fuzzy. Something inside me assumes a defensive posture, because I don't like the pain usually associated with discipline.

Discipline hurts. The word *trained* in today's verse implies suffering, like that experienced by an athlete during preparation for a competition. Unfortunately, God's discipline would prove counter-productive if it were enjoyable. It could never achieve its purpose, that is, repentance. That means it could never convince us to turn from going our own way to going God's way.

When we're heading down the wrong path, God uses both actions and words to get our attention and encourage a change of direction (Hebrews 12:11). Anything he does, he does from a heart of love and concern for our well-being.

Is discipline fun? Never. Therefore, we do ourselves a favor if we respond to our wise heavenly Father immediately versus resisting his efforts or refusing to take them seriously.

Ponder

What's your knee-jerk response to God's discipline?

Pray

God, teach me to view divine discipline not as evidence of your disdain for me but as proof of your delight in me.

> "If I am walking along the street with a very disfiguring hole in the back of my dress, of which I am in ignorance, it is certainly a very great comfort to me to have a kind friend who will tell me of it. And similarly it is indeed a comfort to know that there is always abiding with me a divine, all-seeing Comforter, who will reprove me for all my faults, and will not let me go on in a fatal unconsciousness of them."
>
> HANNAH WHITALL SMITH, *The God of All Comfort*

Treasures

I will give you treasures hidden in the darkness—
secret riches. I will do this so you may know
that I am the LORD, the God of Israel,
the one who calls you by name.

ISAIAH 45:3 NLT

Pause

Sailor-Man and I had anchored in a secluded cove. The next morning dawned with nary a whisper of wind. The water was smooth as glass until, suddenly, dozens of ripples about eighteen inches in diameter broke the surface and began moving toward our vessel.

I peered over the deck rail. That's when I saw it—a nature show that left me in awe. Thousands of teeny fish darted to and fro amidst dozens of jelly-fish in the dark green sea.

Sometimes our life's journey leads to a place of waiting, solitude, or sorrow. It's there we discover treasures we wouldn't find elsewhere: we forge a new friendship, see prayer answered, experience God's promises fulfilled, or discover a new aspect of God's character.

Spiritual treasures hidden in dark places are too precious to miss. Stay alert. Know that God is at work, and he's up to something that just might leave you in awe.

Ponder

What treasures can you see hidden in the darkness?

Pray

God, open my eyes to see the treasures in this place.

"The Bible teaches that true joy is formed in the midst of the difficult seasons of life."

FRANCIS CHAN,
Crazy Love: Overwhelmed by a Relentless God

For Such a Time As This

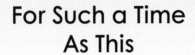

If you keep silent at this time, relief and deliverance
will rise for the Jews from another place,
but you and your father's house will perish.
And who knows whether you have not come
to the kingdom for such a time as this?

ESTHER 4:14 ESV

Pause

Esther was a Jewish teenage orphan exiled to Babylon. The difficult road she'd already walked in her young life grew more challenging when she was taken from everything familiar and placed in the king's harem.

Soon after Esther became queen, one of the king's trusted advisors set a plan in motion to annihilate the Jews. The queen's willingness to plead to the king on their behalf was the Jews' only hope for survival. Esther realized that God had prepared and placed her in the palace for that mission. She found courage to respond, and God granted success.

The phrase "for such a time as this" in Esther's story referred to a specific crisis. If our journey includes stepping into a crisis, we can be sure that God has been preparing us for it. In his providence, he has placed us there for a reason. We're there on purpose—his purpose—for such a time as this.

Ponder

How has God's providence prepared you for a current challenge?

Pray

God, I'm fully available to you for such a time as this.

> "If you align your thoughts and your desires underneath His comprehensive rule over every area of your life, you will walk in peace. He will calm your heart and your mind by giving you peace."
>
> TONY EVANS,
> *Victory in Spiritual Warfare: Outfitting Yourself for the Battle*

Ripples of Joy

*Your love has given me great joy
and encouragement, because you, brother,
have refreshed the hearts of the Lord's people.*

PHILEMON 1:7

Pause

Jane loved Jesus, and her faith motivated her to love others. Volunteering at our church's drop-in center for women became a passion. Her ready smile made ladies of all ages feel welcome, and her readiness to listen made them feel valued and heard.

Everyone who knew Jane grieved deeply when a rare disease claimed her life within weeks of diagnosis. And everyone who knew her agrees that she left a legacy characterized by joy.

Jane possessed joy because she'd found its true source— Jesus. But she didn't keep it to herself. She shared it with others by loving them as Jesus loved her.

The joy that comes from knowing Jesus is impossible to hide or keep to ourselves. It wells within until it bubbles over and splashes on those around us. It's contagious, spread from one person to the next through attitude, word, and deed.

Jane's joy resembled a ripple that began with her faith in Jesus and reached more people than she realized. May we all leave a legacy like hers.

Ponder

Who do you know whose life reflects joy?

Pray

God, deepen my faith in Jesus so that my life will leave ripples of joy reaching far and wide.

> "Keep giving Jesus to your people, not by words, but by your example, by your being in love with Jesus, by radiating his holiness and spreading his fragrance of love everywhere you go. Just keep the joy of Jesus as your strength. Be happy and at peace."
>
> MOTHER TERESA,
> *A Gift for God: Prayers and Meditations*

Sunrise, Sunset

Those who live at the ends of the earth stand in awe
of your wonders. From where the sun rises to
where it sets, you inspire shouts of joy.

PSALM 65:8 NLT

Pause

Watching the sun rise and set is one of my favorite activities when Sailor-Man and I explore west coast islands. Sometimes the sun tinges the sky with soft shades of orange, pink, and yellow. Other times, it sets the heavens ablaze. Either way, the scene stirs a song of praise within me: "Then sings my soul, my Savior God to Thee / How great Thou art, how great Thou art."

Seen around the world, sunrises and sunsets are God's gift to mankind. They remind us of his presence when we wake and before we fall asleep. They point to his power in creating the sun, and his wisdom and knowledge in setting its position in space.

Sunrises and sunsets inspire awe, but they're only tiny glimpses of God's greatness. Let's pause to enjoy them now and again, especially when our journey leads us to a difficult place. As we soak in the sight, let's give thanks that the one responsible for their beauty takes responsibility for us.

Ponder

How does God speak to you through sunrises and sunsets?

Pray

God, the skies declare your greatness. May they inspire songs of joy in me, especially when I feel anything but joyful.

"When you see that sunset or that panoramic view of God's finest expressed in nature, and the beauty just takes your breath away, remember it is just a glimpse of the real thing that awaits you in heaven."

GREG LAURIE,
Every Day with Jesus: Forty Years of Favorite Devotions

An Unexpected Helper

Joyful are those who have the God of Israel as their helper, whose hope is in the LORD their God.

PSALM 146:5 NLT

Pause

Two girlfriends and I waited for our train in Krakow, Poland. Having traveled through this station before, I knew what to expect. Disembarking passengers would have only a few seconds to exit before new passengers would push to board. I'd be caught in the crowd and forced to hustle while lugging my suitcase up several steps into my assigned car. I whispered, "God help me," and prepared for the inevitable.

Suddenly, a little old man dressed in tattered clothes appeared and, using hand motions, offered to carry my suitcase. My Polish girlfriend nodded reassurance, so I agreed. When boarding time arrived, the man moved effortlessly through the crowd and carried my suitcase aboard. He waited until I arrived, tipped his hat, kissed my hand, and left.

God's methods to help us in times of need are infinite and sometimes unexpected. We can never accurately guess how he will answer our prayer for help, but we can be confident that he will fully satisfy our need.

Ponder

For what need are you trusting God to help you?

Pray

God, I look forward to seeing the answer to my prayer for help. Surprise me!

> "Desperation compels us to pray with fervent, focused faith—especially when we have no one else to turn to. God honors our faith when we place it in him alone—with no back-up plan, no other recourse, no other way out. He hears and answers our desperate heart cry, because he loves to show himself strong on our behalf."
>
> ANNE GRAHAM LOTZ, author of *The Daniel Prayer: Prayer That Moves Heaven and Changes Nations*

Praise

Know that the LORD is God. It is he who
made us, and we are his; we are his people,
the sheep of his pasture. Enter his gates with
thanksgiving and his courts with praise;
give thanks to him and praise his name.

PSALM 100:3-4

Pause

"Praise the Lord" is one of Scripture's most repeated commands. God didn't issue it for his sake, to satisfy his ego. He issued it for ours, to turn sorrow to joy when our journey leads through dark valleys.

So why do we praise God when we're on a road we didn't choose? For starters, we praise him because he is God. Our world might feel out of control, but he remains in control.

We praise God for being our creator. We are his masterpieces and delight (Ephesians 2:10; Zephaniah 3:17). Nothing about us and our journey is accidental. We praise him for giving us the privilege of belonging to him. He adopted us and made us his beloved children (Ephesians 1:5). We praise him for being our shepherd and taking responsibility for our well-being (Psalm 23:1).

Praise isn't for God's sake but for ours. It focuses our minds on truth, and the truth sets us free to hold on to hope, even in dark valleys (John 8:32).

Ponder

For what can you praise the Lord today?

Pray

God, thank you for giving me infinite reasons to practice praise no matter what.

> "In the darkest times of your life, your praise to God should be your loudest. Let the enemy know you're not afraid of the dark."
>
> STORMIE OMARTIAN,
> *The Prayer That Changes Everything:*
> *The Hidden Power of Praising God*

Our Citizenship

Our citizenship is in heaven. And we eagerly await
a Savior from there, the Lord Jesus Christ.

PHILIPPIANS 3:20

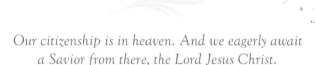

Pause

Sailor-Man and I lead short-term ministry teams to Eastern Europe where we host evangelistic English-learning camps for families. We once invited a co-worker from the Middle East to participate as a youth leader.

The man, in his mid-20s, applied for a visa. He looked forward with anticipation to connecting with teens from another culture and exploring God's Word with them. His dreams were dashed when government officials denied his visa request. Apparently, his age, single status, and nationality flagged him as a potential security threat.

Disappointments abound in this life. So long as we inhabit this world, we'll experience times when our best-laid plans fail or people fail us. But a day is coming when all our disappointments will be forgotten.

Someday we'll receive permanent residency in heaven where our true citizenship lies, and Jesus will welcome us with arms opened wide. He will wipe our tears and banish death, mourning, crying, and pain forever (Revelation 21:4). This promise is true for all whose names are written in the Book of Life, and no one can deny them entry (Revelation 3:5).

Ponder

What personal disappointment will heaven erase?

Pray

God, thank you for guaranteeing residency in your presence for all who believe in Jesus.

> "At death we cross from one territory to another, but we'll have no trouble with visas. Our representative is already there, preparing for our arrival. As citizens of heaven, our entrance is incontestable."
>
> ERWIN W. LUTZER,
> *You're Richer Than You Think*

A Heavenly Perspective

"For my thoughts are not your thoughts,
neither are your ways my ways," declares the LORD.
"As the heavens are higher than the earth,
so are my ways higher than your ways and my
thoughts than your thoughts."

ISAIAH 55:8-9

Pause

The view from an airplane window isn't much to boast about before takeoff. We see concrete, cars, and other planes. Becoming airborne, however, radically changes the view.

Flying on a clear day broadens our understanding of what the world looks like, and we see things we'd never see while grounded. Imagine catching a bird's-eye view of acres of red and yellow tulips while soaring over the Netherlands, thatch-roofed huts sitting on terraced hillsides in Nepal, and massive cracked ice floes off Greenland's coast.

When we face challenges, our human nature sees them from a limited perspective. We cannot possibly grasp the full picture or scope of God's purpose for allowing them, because his thoughts and ways are so much higher than ours. He sees our circumstances from a heavenly perspective—a view we cannot appreciate while grounded.

Someday we'll understand why God allowed or orchestrated certain events in our lives. Until then, let's trust that he knows best.

Ponder

How might God's view of your circumstances differ from yours?

Pray

God, you see details I can't see. My vision is limited from here. I trust your perspective.

> "There will be times when you do not comprehend why [God] allows certain things to occur, and that is to be expected. He is the infinite God while we are limited human creatures. He sees the eternal ramifications of everything that happens. We don't."
>
> HENRY AND RICHARD BLACKABY AND CLAUDE KING,
> *Experiencing God: Knowing and Doing the Will of God*

The God Perspective

*Trust in the LORD with all your heart,
and do not lean on your own understanding.
In all your ways acknowledge him,
and he will make straight your paths.*

PROVERBS 3:5-6 ESV

Pause

The doctor's words "aggressive breast cancer" sent Twila down an unfamiliar path. The diagnosis, prognosis, and treatment options overwhelmed her; but she clung to a promise God gave her: "I will not die but live, and will proclaim what the LORD has done" (Psalm 118:17).

Some days proved more daunting than others. Pain, heartache, and uncertainty dominated Twila's outlook when she fixated on her circumstances. Putting her thoughts back on the Lord and choosing to trust him changed everything. She became more mindful of God's grace, more able to rest in his care, and more aware of his provisions on her road through treatment to recovery.

"Having the God-perspective kept my hope alive," says Twila. Her words apply to all of us when life sends us down an unfamiliar path. We might feel overwhelmed and unable to understand all that's happening, but fixing our thoughts on the Lord and choosing to trust him bring peace and keep hope alive as we walk that path.

Ponder

What's one action you can take to cultivate the God-perspective?

Pray

God, help me not to focus on hardship but to trust in you as we walk this path.

> "I've learned that rather than focusing on what I don't know or understand, I should turn my attention to what I do know. I know God. I know he loves me. I know he's never failed me. I know he wants what's best for me. I choose to trust him and acknowledge him without having to understand everything."
>
> TWILA BELK,
> *The Power to Be: Be Still, Be Grateful, Be Strong, Be Courageous*

Blessings

Every good gift and every perfect gift is from above,
coming down from the Father of lights, with whom
there is no variation or shadow due to change.

JAMES 1:17 ESV

Pause

A dear friend, widowed twice, radiates the joy of the Lord wherever she goes. Hers has been a difficult road, but her faith runs deep, because she keeps her focus on God and his promises. She also keeps a daily gratitude journal. Recording the things for which she's thankful, she says, has helped heal her hurting heart.

My friend's enthusiasm for her journal inspired me to begin the same practice. At first, I noted the obvious: health, food, and shelter. But then the list began to grow—sunshine, my morning coffee, a FaceTime call with my kids, a tea party with a two-year-old, a birthday lunch with a neighbor, wildflowers growing along the path where I walk. One day, I felt especially grateful for the marina's laundromat being available when I needed to wash our clothes.

It's easy to overlook God's blessings, but taking time to acknowledge them on paper awakens us to the reality of his goodness, especially when we're traveling a difficult road.

Ponder

What are three things you could write in a gratitude journal today?

Pray

God, I give you thanks for every blessing you bring my way.

> "Seek, as a plain duty, to cultivate a buoyant joyous sense of the crowded kindnesses of God in your daily life."
>
> ALEXANDER MACLAREN,
> *Expositions of Holy Scripture: Psalms*

Fear

God has not given us a spirit of fear and timidity,
but of power, love, and self-discipline.

2 TIMOTHY 1:7 NLT

Pause

The Bible addresses fear more than 350 times, because God knows it's a big deal for us. Letting it control our thoughts always affects our behavior and leads to a negative outcome. The Israelites' response to the ten spies' report offers one example of this.

Moses sent twelve spies to scope out the promised land. They returned with good news and bad news. Ten of them focused on the latter, and their fear of defeat spread to the entire population who then wept all night and rebelled against Moses. In the end, the land flowing with milk and honey was rejected, God sent the Israelites on a forty-year journey through the wilderness (Numbers 13–14), and the ten spies died along with almost an entire generation of Israelites.

Focusing on negative what-ifs can lead to an outcome much different from what God wants for us. Let's learn from the Israelites' experience and not let fear lead us into wandering in a wilderness. Instead, let's take hold of God's promises and live as though we believe they're true so that we can enjoy the abundant life God intends.

Ponder

What fear tries to control your thoughts?

Pray

God, take control of my thoughts and make your promises a bigger deal than fear.

"You might categorize your own fear as anxiety. But while the reality of fear is different for each of us, one thing remains constant: fear robs us of joy. When fear takes center stage, we find it impossible to live in the 'what is' because of the 'what might be.'"

SHEILA WALSH, *The Storm Inside: Trade the Chaos of How You Feel for the Truth of Who You Are*

Sleep in Peace

In peace I will both lie down and sleep;
for you alone, O lord, make me dwell in safety.

PSALM 4:8 ESV

Pause

Traveling for ministry purposes means I often stay in hotels. That's fine when Sailor-Man is with me, but it's a different story when I'm alone. Especially at bedtime. What-if thoughts creep in, and fear follows close behind. They switch my brain to high alert, and sleep becomes sporadic.

Maybe you don't often stay in unfamiliar places, but you lose sleep in your own home. Fear and worry can hold us captive anywhere, if we allow them to take up residence in our minds. So what's the solution?

When what-ifs come to mind, I rein them in and replace them with God's Word. I commit my concerns to the Lord, thank him for carrying them on my behalf, and then meditate on a familiar Bible verse until I fall asleep (Philippians 4:6–8).

Nighttime makes us vulnerable to the enemy of our soul, and he always attacks our thoughts. Focusing our minds on truth defeats his tactics. Peace replaces fear and worry, and we're able to enjoy a good night's sleep.

Ponder

What thoughts keep you awake at night?

Pray

God, grant me the ability to train my mind to think on your truth—especially during the night hours.

"It says in [Philippians 4] verse 7, 'the peace of God ... will guard your hearts and your minds.' The Greek word translated as 'guard' means to completely surround and fortify a building or a city to protect it from invasion. If you have an army all around you protecting you, then you can sleep really well—that's the idea."

TIMOTHY KELLER,
Walking with God through Pain and Suffering

A Little Bit of Hope

*Yes, my soul, find rest in God; my hope comes
from him. Truly he is my rock and my salvation;
he is my fortress, I will not be shaken.*

PSALM 62:5–6

Pause

The storm began for Quanny and her family when their
tenant stopped paying rent. Her husband's sudden job
loss two months later increased its intensity. The COVID-19
shutdown hit immediately afterward and thrust them into a
perfect storm. When her husband found a job in a different
state, they had no option but to pack their belongings, say
goodbye to everything familiar, and relocate.

So much loss in so little time and without warning broke
Quanny's heart. Her family's inability to truly settle into their
new community due to pandemic restrictions added to
her pain. She felt this was the hardest year of their life, and
there seemed to be no end in sight; but she hung on to
hope—albeit by a thread. In Quanny's words, "That little
bit was just enough."

Sometimes that little bit is all we have, but it provides courage to carry on. It whispers reminders that God is with us, and it gives us the settled assurance that everything will somehow, someday be okay.

Ponder

How have you experienced hope while waiting for a storm to end?

Pray

God, thank you for giving me all the hope I need for this day.

> "Hope doesn't have to be a grand or spectacular display or even exist in vast amounts. For me, hope was a lifeline thrown out in a sea of uncertainty, doubt, fear, and pain. It allowed me to break the surface of the relentless waves of grief long enough to see God's goodness and to believe that goodness was for me despite the hardships we faced."
>
> QUANTRILLA ARD, *The PhD Mamma*

Cling to God

Serve only the LORD your God
and fear him alone. Obey his commands,
listen to his voice, and cling to him.

DEUTERONOMY 13:4 NLT

Pause

Sea creatures flourish in the pristine environment around Vancouver Island's southern tip. One morning, I visited a dock in that area at low tide. The posts, or pilings, that held the dock in place towered above the water's surface. Purple starfish of all sizes covered them. I tried to pry a starfish free but failed. It clung to the piling with a grip that surprised me.

God seeks our well-being, so he commands us to cling to him. The enemy of our soul tries to pry our grip loose. He uses discouragement and fear to instill doubt about who God is. In place of God, he offers modern-day idols such as money, ministry, family, reputation, and pleasures. He even uses our insecurities—perfectionism and the need for others' approval—to force us to let go of God. Be aware of his methods and do not succumb.

Cling to the Lord when temptation knocks, my friend. Hold tight to him when hardships come. Read his Word, converse with him, invite his presence into every part of life, and obey his commands so that all may go well with you.

Ponder

To what are you clinging for security?

Pray

God, loosen my grip on anything that prevents me from clinging to you as my sole source of wisdom, strength, joy, and peace.

> "If God allows you to wrestle with him, it is not so there will be a winner and a loser. He doesn't need to prove he is stronger and you are weaker. No. The point of wrestling with God is to give you an opportunity to cling to him. God wants you to hang on to him no matter what—and the result will be blessing."
>
> JENNIFER ROTHSCHILD, *God Is Just Not Fair: Finding Hope When Life Doesn't Make Sense*

God's Hands

I hold you by your right hand—
I, the LORD your God. And I say to you,
"Don't be afraid. I am here to help you."

ISAIAH 41:13 NLT

Pause

Sailor-Man and I took our eighteen-month-old granddaughter, Lexi, to the zoo. Carefree and happy for independence, she toddled between us on the wide, paved path. All went well until the zoo's mini-train approached and the engineer clanged its brass bell.

The noise startled Lexi, and she instinctively grabbed for my hand. She visibly relaxed the moment I responded. She felt safe with Grandma's hand holding hers.

The Lord knows that his children are often easily frightened, so he reassures us of his presence and says he holds our right hand. Think about the magnitude of this promise. These are the hands that shaped the universe (Psalm 19:1); they led the Israelites from Egypt into the promised land

(Jeremiah 32:21); and they were punctured by nails on our behalf (John 20:27).

The hand that holds ours is infinitely stronger than Grandma's. If Lexi could relax when I held her hand, then surely we can rest knowing the Lord our God holds ours.

Ponder

What picture comes to mind when you think of God holding your hand?

Pray

God, I'm slipping my hand into yours today. Please hold tight and don't let me go.

"Contentment should be the hallmark of my life, as I put my affairs in the hands of God."

W. PHILLIP KELLER,
*The Lord Is My Shepherd: Reflections from
A Shepherd Looks at Psalm 23*

Beauty from Brokenness

*[Jesus] said to her, "Daughter, your faith
has made you well; go in peace."*

LUKE 8:48 ESV

Pause

The woman had exhausted every hope for healing.
Numerous doctors had examined her and given the same
prognosis: "Your condition has no cure." Their words left her
feeling broken beyond repair. She would spend the rest of
her life dealing with a physical issue that weakened her
body and rendered her untouchable, like a leper.

Everything changed when the woman's journey led her
to Jesus, the one who brings beauty from brokenness.
He healed her body, but he also healed her soul.
Within earshot of all who despised her, Jesus called her
"daughter," a term of endearment and of relationship.
He commended her for her faith, and then he blessed her
with *shalom*—peace—and with wholeness in every part
of her being (Luke 8:43–48).

Do you feel broken? Run to Jesus for help. He knows your situation better than anyone, he knows how you feel, and he knows how to turn the broken pieces of your life into beauty. Trust him, and let him make you whole again.

Ponder

What's broken? Your health? Career aspirations? A relationship? Something else?

Pray

God, craft my brokenness into beauty, not only for my benefit, but for your sake and the sake of your kingdom.

> "If you find yourself right now in a place where you are heartbroken, I want to remind you that Christ is very close to the broken. Our culture throws broken things away, but our Savior never does. He gently gathers all the pieces, and with His love and in His time, He puts us back together."
>
> SHEILA WALSH, *The Storm Inside: Trade the Chaos of How You Feel for the Truth of Who You Are*

Let It Go

Give all your worries and cares to God,
for he cares about you.

1 PETER 5:7 NLT

Pause

Christin sat in the audience at a women's conference. Her smile conveyed confidence and joy, but she wore it like a mask to hide the hurt inside. Everything in her life was spinning out of control—her control—and she couldn't fix it. It wasn't for lack of trying. She'd done everything possible to pull things back together for friends and family, but nothing had worked.

Christin listened as the speaker told of her toddler receiving a helium balloon with a string attached. She told him to hold the string tight, but he did the opposite. When she asked why he released it, he said, "I didn't let it go, Mommy! I gave it to Jesus."

The story moved Christin to tears. She'd believed that letting go of her loved ones' problems meant she was abandoning those for whom she deeply cared. The balloon illustration helped her understand that letting go meant she was not turning her back on them; she was giving them to Jesus. He had the answers, and he—not she—could care best for their needs.

Ponder

What balloon of care do you need to give to Jesus?

Pray

God, I give up trying to control things that aren't mine to control. I let go and give them to you.

"There are so many things we just can't control. The answer is 'let it go.' But the only way we can really let go is if we're giving it to Jesus....
We're entrusting them to the Creator of All Things. To the One who is so much wiser, so much stronger, so much more resourceful, so much more just and good and patient and loving and kind. He knows what to do, so much better than we do."

CHRISTIN DITCHFIELD, *What Women Should Know about Letting It Go: Breaking Free from the Power of Guilt, Discouragement, and Defeat*

Renewal

Even youths shall faint and be weary, and young men
shall fall exhausted; but they who wait for the L ORD
shall renew their strength; they shall mount up with
wings like eagles; they shall run and not be weary;
they shall walk and not faint.

ISAIAH 40:30–31 ESV

Pause

Sometimes our journey places extra demands on our physical, emotional, and mental energy. Left with little reserve, we feel weary from the inside out. In times like these, we find our strength renewed by waiting on God.

Waiting does not mean we sit still and expect God to infuse us with doses of fresh energy. It means being twisted together with him. As fibers are twisted together to make a strong, useful rope, we twist ourselves together with God by taking intentional actions to focus on him. We seek him through his Word, converse with him in prayer, fill our minds with praise and worship music, and invite him into every part of our day.

The God of infinite power renews our strength as we draw close to him. We come empty, and he fills us in a way that nothing else can.

Ponder

What actions have you taken to renew your strength in the past? How did that work for you?

Pray

God, teach me to wait on you when I'm weary.

> "We can be tired, weary, and emotionally distraught,
> but after spending time alone with God,
> we find that He injects into our bodies energy,
> power, and strength."
>
> CHARLES STANLEY, *How to Listen to God*

Friends

It is the LORD who goes before you.
He will be with you; he will not leave you
or forsake you. Do not fear or be dismayed.

DEUTERONOMY 31:8 ESV

Pause

Sailor-Man and I enjoy practicing hospitality aboard our sailboat whether we're tied to our dock or anchored offshore. So when one of our neighbors told us that he planned to take a trip that would place him in our vicinity while we were offshore, we promised to meet him for an evening.

The day our paths merged, we anchored our boats side by side and tied them together. He and his two buddies came aboard for dinner and again for breakfast the next day. We lingered over coffee before untying the ropes and going our separate ways.

Human friendships are great, but they're far different from our friendship with Jesus. He doesn't set his schedule to meet us in a prearranged place on a certain day, pop in for a visit, and then leave us. He travels with us everywhere we go. He never leaves our side.

Imagine two sailboats tied together traveling from one destination to the next. That's what friendship with Jesus looks like.

Ponder

What picture comes to mind when you think about your friendship with Jesus?

Pray

God, thank you for staying by my side on this journey.

> "The dearest friend on earth is a mere shadow compared to Jesus Christ."
>
> OSWALD CHAMBERS,
> *Studies in the Sermon on the Mount*

Rejoice

Rejoice in the Lord always.
I will say it again: Rejoice!

PHILIPPIANS 4:4

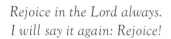

Pause

We all face two potential joy-stealers: difficult circumstances and difficult relationships. The apostle Paul addressed our best defense against them: "Rejoice!"

First, Paul taught that joy is rooted not in happy circumstances but in our understanding of the Lord's faithfulness and control over our lives. Because these things never change, we have reason to rejoice, no matter where our journey takes us. Paul practiced what he preached, for he wrote this letter while in prison for his faith.

Next, Paul implied that rejoicing in the Lord helps us navigate difficult relationships. We know this is true because he wrote today's key verse after urging two female co-laborers to set their differences aside and for other believers to help them reconcile (Philippians 4:2–9).

Rejoicing in the Lord helps us keep our minds on what matters most. There's no room for petty annoyances to take up residence when the things of God dwell in our thoughts. Jealousy, envy, criticism, and unforgiveness cannot share the same space as God's love and peace.

When our journey leads to a difficult place or relationship, let's recall and put into practice Paul's teaching wrapped in one little word: *rejoice*.

Ponder

About what aspect of God's character can you rejoice today?

Pray

God, teach me to rejoice in your faithfulness and sovereignty, no matter where my journey takes me.

> "Begin to rejoice in the Lord, and your bones will flourish like an herb, and your cheeks will glow with the bloom of health and freshness. Worry, fear, distrust, care are all poison drops; joy is balm and healing, and if you will but rejoice, God will give power."
>
> A. B. SIMPSON, *Days of Heaven upon Earth: A Year Book of Scripture Texts and Living Truths*

Real-Life Struggles

Let us … [fix] our eyes on Jesus, the pioneer and perfecter of faith. For the joy set before him he endured the cross, scorning its shame, and sat down at the right hand of the throne of God.

HEBREWS 12:1-2

Pause

Nancie and her husband decided to take a highly recommended hike. They began second-guessing their decision after trudging four miles uphill through dense forest on a path that seemed to lead nowhere.

All doubts disappeared when the path led to a meadow teeming with wildflowers watered by glacier-fed streams. The couple sat by a stream and ate their lunch, savoring the mountaintop experience. All too soon, they had to leave the idyllic scene to start their long hike homeward.

We love our mountaintop experiences and wish we could linger there, but real life beckons. Sometimes our life path feels tedious and exhausting. Some days we wonder whether what we do matters. We might look at the path we're walking and question whether it's worth the energy it demands.

Hang on to hope, my friend. God walks with you, and he will lead you to a beautiful place—a place of sweet intimacy with himself, a place reached only through real-life struggles.

Ponder

What reward have you experienced through perseverance?

Pray

God, grant me strength and endurance until I reach the joy you've set before me.

"Remember that there are songs yet to be sung. Paintings yet to be created. Books yet to be written. Lives to be touched for God. Families to be forged. Marriages to be crafted. Lives of integrity yet to be lived. For you to attain these things, you must persevere, stay on the path, and allow God's Word to light your way (see Psalm 119:105)."

NANCIE CARMICHAEL, *The Comforting Presence of God*

Hardships Happen

*Dear friends, do not be surprised at the fiery
ordeal that has come on you to test you, as though
something strange were happening to you.*

1 PETER 4:12

Pause

Sailor-Man and I traveled frequently on public buses when
we lived in Nepal. We soon realized that every bus came
with a mechanic—and for good reason: drivers always
anticipated a breakdown of some sort. No journey was
complete without one, so they went prepared.

In a similar way, we ought to anticipate times of suffering
along our life's journey. Anyone who claims that Christ's
followers never have problems speaks untruth. Don't be
fooled. The truth is, hardships happen. Expect them.

That said, we don't spend our days wringing our hands
and staring at the horizon, waiting for the next storm cloud
to appear. Rather, we prepare ourselves by studying
God's Word and spending time in his presence. We meet

with other believers to learn and grow spiritually. We get involved wherever God leads us. We prepare ourselves for the inevitable, so we can face it victoriously when it comes.

Let's be neither anxious about hardships in advance nor surprised when they arise. But let's be ready to face them and learn from them when they come.

Ponder

What's your first response when you encounter a hardship?

Pray

God, thank you for the heads-up about hardships. Prepare my heart for what you know lies ahead.

"God does not say, 'If you go through the fire' and flood and dark valleys but *when* you go. The promise is not that he will remove us from the experience of suffering. No, the promise is that God will be with us, walking beside us in it."

TIMOTHY KELLER,
Walking with God through Pain and Suffering

Suffering

In all this you greatly rejoice, though now for a little while you may have had to suffer grief in all kinds of trials. These have come so that the proven genuineness of your faith—of greater worth than gold, which perishes even though refined by fire—may result in praise, glory and honor when Jesus Christ is revealed.

1 PETER 1:6-7

Pause

When someone suffers tragedy, we often hear, "There must be a reason." Indeed, there *is* a reason. Our God is too loving, kind, and wise to bring us grief just because. That's not his nature. When he allows suffering, we can be confident he has a purpose.

One reason God allows suffering is to refine and prove our faith true. Anyone can claim to possess faith, but what happens to said faith when God turns up the heat? Does it melt into nothingness, or does it grow stronger and purer?

God proves our faith for our sake, not his. Discovering it's stronger than expected encourages us in our faith journey. Discovering its weaknesses spurs us on to growth. The only way to reveal what's what is to test our faith, and suffering is the best means to do that.

Ponder

What's one thing you've discovered about your faith through suffering?

Pray

God, you know that suffering hurts because you suffered, too. I'm grateful that the purpose for your pain was to free me from mine.

"I believe that suffering is part of the narrative, and that nothing really good gets built when everything's easy. I believe that loss and emptiness and confusion often give way to new fullness and wisdom."

SHAUNA NIEQUIST,
*Bittersweet: Thoughts on Change, Grace,
and Learning the Hard Way*

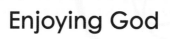

Enjoying God

*Take delight in the L*ORD*, and he will
give you the desires of your heart.*

PSALM 37:4

Pause

As children of God, our duty is to love and respect God as he deserves. We're to surrender our will to him and serve him by doing whatever he commands. These aspects of our relationship with him are good and necessary, but let's remember to enjoy him, too.

Enjoying the Lord does not denote a casual, buddy-buddy relationship in which we lower him to peer level. It means we look to him more than any earthly pleasure or person to satisfy our deepest longings. We delight in learning about him and in developing intimacy with him through obedience, prayer, and reading his Word. We crave his nearness, so we invite his presence into every part of our day.

Learning to enjoy God reframes and refreshes our faith journey. In all we say and do, we're motivated by love for him, rather than an unhealthy fear of him. Inner peace replaces an incessant striving for perfection. Rest replaces restlessness.

God created us to know him, but he also created us to enjoy him. That's an important but often overlooked aspect of our faith journey.

Ponder

What's one thing you enjoy about God?

Pray

God, please grant my heart's desire to know and enjoy you.

> "Enjoying God is all about intimacy with God.
> It's about knowing Him and being known by Him.
> It's experiencing His love and responding to it.
> It's serving Him out of a sincere desire to please Him
> because he is the supreme pleasure of your life."
>
> S. J. HILL, *Enjoying God: Experiencing Intimacy with the Heavenly Father*

Joyful Disruptions

*There is more joy in heaven over one lost sinner who
repents and returns to God than over ninety-nine
others who are righteous and haven't strayed away!*

LUKE 15:7 NLT

Pause

Sailor-Man and I were traveling into Romania by train. At the border, several guards examined our passports, motioned for us to gather our belongings, and led us off the train to a nearby police station.

Inside, an English-speaking officer questioned us for more than an hour about our travel itinerary. Finally, she assigned a guard to watch us and then disappeared with our passports.

The guard, speaking broken English, began asking personal questions. Our conversation rolled naturally into talking about Jesus and the hope he brings. Minutes later, the lead officer returned, apologized for the confusion, and freed us to leave.

That experience disrupted our travel plans. It was a hassle and a bit unnerving but necessary. God had prepared the guard's heart to hear the good news about Jesus, and God needed us there to deliver the message.

If God disrupts our plans to give us opportunity to stir joy in heaven, then who are we to complain?

Ponder

When circumstances beyond your control have disrupted your plans, has your response ended up being a blessing for someone?

Pray

God, reframe my thinking about disruptions. Use them to bless others and build your kingdom.

> "The Christian life is a pilgrimage from earth to heaven, and our task is to take as many as possible with us as we make this journey."
>
> WARREN W. WIERSBE, *A Gallery of Grace:*
> *Twelve New Testament Pictures of the Christian Life*

God Provides

Don't worry about these things, saying,
"What will we eat? What will we drink?
What will we wear?" Seek the Kingdom of God
above all else, and live righteously,
and he will give you everything you need.

MATTHEW 6:31, 33 NLT

Pause

I'd been scheduled to speak at a one-day conference in Iowa and chose to travel light, using only a carry-on suitcase. As my departing flight boarded, the gate attendant announced that the overhead bins were full. "Check your bags at the bottom of the gangway," she said. I followed her instructions.

I arrived at my destination, but my suitcase did not. After an initial moment of panic, I explained my situation to my hostess who then drove me to a store to buy a few necessities. She also asked the owner of a women's clothing shop to bring several outfits to my hotel room. "Choose the one you want to wear," she said with a smile.

I smiled, too, because the outfit I wore the next day was more attractive and comfortable than the one I'd packed.

God knows our needs and is more than able to meet them. Let's not stress. Instead, let's watch with joyful anticipation to see how he'll provide.

Ponder

Identify a current physical need (not a want) you're experiencing.

Pray

God, I lack, but you do not. I trust you to provide everything I need today and every day.

> "One of the names of God is Jehovah Jireh, which means 'the Lord our provider' or 'the Lord will provide.' It's so wonderful to know that God is our source for everything we need and He cares about everything we care about. There's no need so small that He doesn't know about it, and nothing too big that He can't provide for us."
>
> JOYCE MEYER

A New Path

When you see the ark of the covenant of the LORD
your God, and the Levitical priests carrying it,
you are to move out from your positions and follow it.
Then you will know which way to go,
since you have never been this way before.

JOSHUA 3:3-4

Pause

After wandering the wilderness for forty years, the time had finally come for the Israelites to cross into the promised land. The prospect of leaving everything familiar behind must have felt daunting.

God knew how his people felt. He also knew their tendency to fear and to fail at following his commands. So to help them succeed in the new venture, he put a strategy in place: He sent the Ark of the Covenant—the dwelling place of God—ahead of the people. This way, they didn't need to figure out the route on which to travel. They only needed to follow him.

God uses the same strategy today. We might feel afraid when our circumstances change and take us down a new path. The good news is that God doesn't expect us to figure out the route on our own. He goes before us and his presence leads the way. We only have to follow.

Ponder

How do you feel when changing circumstances put you on an unfamiliar path?

Pray

God, please help me follow you fearlessly into new territory.

"I don't have to figure out *why* or *how* or *when*. God has a plan, and I'm committed to it. That commitment frees me from having to worry about the details."

BARBARA JOHNSON,
Amazing Freedom: Devotions to Free Your Spirit and Fill Your Heart

When Plans Change

The heart of man plans his way,
but the LORD establishes his steps.

PROVERBS 16:9 ESV

Pause

Sailor-Man and I have discovered that taking a boat trip requires a ton of planning. For instance, we schedule our departure based on the tide. If it's too low, our keel will get stuck in the muddy river bottom. We schedule our arrival at the river's mouth to avoid wild waves created when the tide changes direction. We estimate how far we can travel in a day and where we should anchor for the night.

We make plans, but circumstances beyond our control can change things in a heartbeat. Bad weather and boat breakdowns top the list. Experience has taught us to be flexible. We commit each day to the Lord and then refuse to stress when the unexpected happens.

It's wise to adopt the same response for our life's journey. We make plans, but then stuff happens over which we have no control. Let's commit each new day to the Lord and remember that he is sovereign, wise, and good. He's in control, so we don't need to be. We only need to trust him and refuse to stress.

Ponder

What's your usual response when stuff happens beyond your control?

Pray

God, I'll write my best-laid plans in pencil and willingly erase them when you change them.

"I can face things that are out of my control
and not act out of control."

LYSA TERKEURST,
Unglued: Making Wise Choices in the Midst of Raw Emotions

Beneficial Words

Do not let any unwholesome talk come out of
your mouths, but only what is helpful for
building others up according to their needs,
that it may benefit those who listen.

EPHESIANS 4:29

Pause

Karen's discipleship group of young teen girls organized an evening event and invited a guest speaker. They assumed responsibility for setting up tables and chairs before the meeting began.

When Karen arrived, she discovered that they'd arranged nothing according to plan. She was just about to say something regrettable when the girls opened the stage curtains and yelled, "Surprise!"

Karen swallowed her words and stared at a pile of presents. Without her knowledge, the girls had bumped the planned event into the following week, so they could bless her with a baby shower for her soon-to-be-born child.

Understandably, Karen was grateful she hadn't squelched the girls' joy with her words.

We so easily say things that wound, deflate, and discourage when we're overtired or we feel others fall short of our expectations. Our words carry power, so let's use them wisely, okay? We don't always know what another person's journey is like, so let's choose words that empower, encourage, and inspire joy.

Ponder

How have you inspired joy in someone's life through words?

Pray

God, take control of my mouth, so the words I speak will bless others.

"Words, like hope, begin in your heart.
A hopeful person speaks with gentleness and love
that sprinkle kindness and joy into people's lives."

KAREN WHITING,
365 Devotions for Hope

Run the Race

Since we are surrounded by so great
a cloud of witnesses, let us also lay aside
every weight, and sin which clings so closely,
and let us run with endurance
the race that is set before us.

HEBREWS 12:1 ESV

Pause

My youngest daughter ran long-distance races in her teen years. Sometimes she ran on school tracks, but often she raced on forest trails. The latter, especially, demanded undivided focus. She learned to lay aside distracting thoughts and to concentrate on the path to prevent tripping or twisting an ankle on uneven ground. Her efforts paid off, and she always finished well.

You and I are running a long-distance race, too. Our paths look different from one another's, but they all warrant our undivided focus. If we hope to endure and finish well, we must lay aside those things that hinder us.

Unbelief is a common hindrance that affects our progress. Doubting God's goodness, wisdom, and power paralyzes us. The good news is that the heroes of the faith shed unbelief and ran their race by faith in God's promises. They endured and finished strong, and we can do the same.

Ponder

What's one weight you must set aside, so you can endure the race set before you?

Pray

God, help me run the race before me with faith in my heart and the Spirit to guide me in the way I should go.

"There is nothing that God expects you to do that you cannot do. The sin that defeats you need not defeat you. The fears that consume you need not consume you. The people who terrify you need not terrify you."

TIM CHESTER,
Enjoying God: Experiencing the Power and Love of God in Everyday Life

Give Thanks

Give thanks to the lord, for he is good;
his love endures forever.

PSALM 107:1

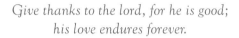

When Sailor-Man and I visited ministry coworkers in Egypt, we rented accommodations in their neighborhood. Far from the tourist district, I rose early one morning and stepped onto our seventh-floor balcony. On a rooftop below, I saw a half-naked boy about ten years old exit a cardboard box, stretch, and then crawl back inside. I saw him on a couple other occasions, but he was always alone. An orphan simply trying to survive?

This child's situation broke my heart. It also humbled me, for seeing the boy's existence reminded me that my life is easier than most of the world's population, even on days I consider difficult.

God wants us to give thanks in all circumstances. Doing so is easy when life's easy, but not so much when we face challenges. When we're hard-pressed to feel thankful, let's go back to the basics and express gratitude for blessings close at hand: food and clean drinking water, hot showers, housing, clothes, and family. Joy comes when we do as a well-known song suggests: "Count [our] blessings, name them one by one."

Ponder

Identify three blessings you enjoy but which most of the world does not experience.

Pray

God, thank you for the basics and so much more.

> "Joy ... has nothing to do with material things or with our outward circumstances.... Someone living in the lap of luxury can be wretched and someone else who is in the depths of poverty can overflow with joy."
>
> WILLIAM BARCLAY,
> *The New Daily Bible Study: The Letters to the Philippians, Colossians, and Thessalonians*

The Upside of Pain

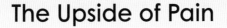

*[God] said [to Paul], "My grace is all
you need. My power works best in weakness."
So now I am glad to boast about my weaknesses,
so that the power of Christ can work through me.*

2 CORINTHIANS 12:9 NLT

Pause

A physical affliction tormented the apostle Paul. He asked God three times to remove it, but God had a different plan: he left the problem but provided Paul with everything needed to deal with it.

God poured his grace—his love and favor—onto Paul. He poured his divine power into him. God's infinite, generous supply of grace and power strengthened Paul to fulfill his call. The chronic thorn in the flesh bore a constant reminder of his dependence on God. Rather than chafe over his weakened state, he rejoiced in it.

We'd prefer suffering to not cross our path, but sometimes God has a different plan. If his purpose for us involves pain, then he will provide everything we need to deal with it. He will give us the power to fulfill our call or the perseverance needed to adapt to a new normal. Heaven forbid we chafe over our weakness when, in reality, it's the portal through which God's power flows.

Ponder

Identify a perceived weakness in your life, physical or otherwise.

Pray

God, help me see my weakness as the portal through which your power flows.

"Suffering is seldom an item on our list of requests to the Lord. But when it crosses our path and we are able by His grace to keep on walking, our lives become messages of hope to the world and to the church."

SHEILA WALSH, *Life Is Tough, but God Is Faithful: How to See God's Love in Difficult Times*

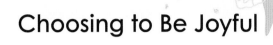

Choosing to Be Joyful

Even though the fig trees have no blossoms, and there are no grapes on the vines; even though the olive crop fails, and the fields lie empty and barren; even though the flocks die in the fields, and the cattle barns are empty, yet I will rejoice in the LORD! I will be joyful in the God of my salvation!

HABAKKUK 3:17–18 NLT

Pause

Following her high school graduation, our oldest daughter, Stephanie, chose to attend Bible college in Alberta. Sailor-Man and I supported her decision, but as missionaries dependent on donations for income, we weren't sure how we'd cover college expenses.

Fear about finances soared when our car's transmission blew an hour after we left home to deliver Stephanie to college. The next day, I broke a molar and faced a hefty dental bill. Two days after that, our mechanic said our tires were threadbare and needed to be replaced immediately.

I cried and questioned God's intent toward us. We considered getting a "real" job. Finally, frustrated with increasing feelings of negativity, I chose to shift my focus from financial fears to God's faithfulness. Doing so didn't cancel the bills, but it calmed my concerns and restored my joy.

Ponder

Complete this declaration: Even though _____, I will choose to rejoice in the Lord's faithfulness.

Pray

God, I chose joy today because you are faithful no matter what.

> "Praising God and trusting Him should not ... fluctuate with our situation. Conditions may change, but God remains steadfast. He may not remove your problems, but He will keep His hand on you. So choose to rejoice. After all, God is ever faithful."
>
> HENRY AND RICHARD BLACKABY,
> *Being Still with God Every Day: A 366 Daily Devotional*

Waiting on God

Wait for the LORD; be strong, and let your heart take courage; wait for the LORD!

PSALM 27:14 ESV

Pause

Scholars believe David was about twenty years old when Samuel anointed him as Israel's next king (1 Samuel 16:13). Ten years passed before David began his reign.

Waiting a decade to assume his rightful position was no small feat for David, but he made the most of it. He learned military strategies. He accomplished victories that established him as a leader. He served Saul and honored him, even when the jealous king tried to kill him. When the time was right and David was ready, God put him on the throne.

Waiting for God to fulfill his promises or open doors of opportunity isn't easy, but it's the better way. We might think it's a time-waster, but God sees it as necessary and productive. He uses it to refine and prepare us for what lies ahead, just as he used David's decade to shape him into a man of might and integrity.

Waiting for God is not something to be merely endured. It's part of his process to accomplish his purposes, so let's embrace it and make the most of it.

Ponder

For what are you waiting on God? How are you dealing with it?

Pray

God, give me patience as I wait for you to fulfill your purposes in my life.

> "Our focus is often on the wait; God's focus is on the work. Through the process of the wait, we have the privilege of relying on him by choosing to read and believe his Word. Poised at opportunity's edge, we learn to listen to his direction by trusting that our Creator desires the best for us. Standing still, listening to his voice, and having our hearts open to his Word— these waiting activities provide and build strength."
>
> RACHEL WOJO, *One More Step:*
> *Finding Strength When You Feel Like Giving Up*

Sowing Seeds

Those who plant in tears will harvest with shouts of joy. They weep as they go to plant their seed, but they sing as they return with the harvest.

PSALM 126:5-6 NLT

Pause

Life looked anything but normal for Sophie after her husband lost his battle with cancer. She'd always risen early and approached each day with gusto, but now she struggled to crawl from bed and cried while doing routine tasks. She'd always enjoyed cooking, but now food held no appeal. Watching her kids wrestle with their own grief compounded hers, but it motivated her to keep going—to put one foot in front of the next and then the next.

One evening, Sophie made popcorn as the kids watched a movie. Suddenly, she heard them erupt in laughter. The sound seemed foreign but, oh, so sweet. That's the moment she knew her family would heal.

Life really hurts sometimes, but God gives us the strength to sow our seeds amid tears—to put one foot in front of the next and then the next. Hang on to hope, my friend. Harvest will come in due season, and your tear-drenched seeds will bear buds of joy.

Ponder

What seeds are you sowing in tears during this season?

Pray

God, I trust you to bring forth a rich harvest from the seeds I'm soaking with my tears.

> "Sowing is simply the work that has to be done even when there are things in life that make us cry. The crops won't wait while we finish our grief or solve all our problems. If we are going to eat next winter, we must get out in the field and sow the seed whether we are crying or not. [Psalm 126] teaches the tough truth that there is work to be done whether I am emotionally up for it or not; and it is good for me to do it."
>
> JOHN PIPER, A Godward Life:
> Seeing the Supremacy of God in All of Life

Joy Is a Choice

As for me, I will sing about your power.
Each morning I will sing with joy
about your unfailing love.

PSALM 59:16 NLT

Pause

Our trip to Slovakia began well, meaning that we arrived at the airport on time. It ended well, too, meaning we arrived at our final destination with suitcases in tow. But everything got muddled in the middle.

The airline canceled the first leg of our journey as we stood at the boarding gate, so we had to reschedule for the next available flight. This was no small feat, as two hundred other passengers clamored to do the same.

Our connecting flight in Toronto was already boarding when we landed, so we raced through the city-size airport to our gate. The last passengers to arrive, we fell breathless and sweaty into our seats. That's when the pilot announced that takeoff would be delayed approximately one hour.

Sailor-Man and I didn't know whether to laugh or cry over the day's events. We *did*, however, know that our response in the moment would determine our attitude for the remainder of the trip. We whispered a prayer of thanks that we'd made our connection—with time to spare—and settled in for the ride.

Ponder

How do you respond to inconveniences and hassles?

Pray

God, help me to choose joy, even when circumstances tempt me to choose otherwise.

> "This next sentence is one of the most important spiritual truths you will ever learn: God develops the fruit of the Spirit in your life by allowing you to experience circumstances in which you're tempted to express the *exact opposite quality!* Character development always involves a choice, and temptation provides that opportunity."
>
> RICK WARREN, *The Purpose Driven Life: What on Earth Am I Here For?*

God Answers

Call to me and I will answer you,
and will tell you great and hidden things
that you have not known.

JEREMIAH 33:3 ESV

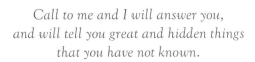

Pause

An electronic message on our boat's control board warned of battery trouble as we prepared to head home after a three-week sailing trip. Memories of a terrifying adventure on the water the year before came to mind like a flash flood. It began with—you guessed it—battery trouble.

"What should we do?" I asked Sailor-Man. "I'm not sure," he said. He fiddled with several switches on the panel board, and I prayed. "Father, we don't know what the problem is, but you do. Please show us what's wrong."

Moments later, the electronic message indicated that the problem was resolved. "That was easy," said Sailor-Man. "I realized that I'd forgotten to push *that* button."

God's knowledge far supersedes ours. When we face a problem for which we have no solution, rest assured he knows the answer. Sometimes he shares it with us immediately; other times, he has us wait. Our role is to call to him for help. His role is to answer, and he will—in the manner and time he knows is best.

Ponder

Imagine the vastness of God's unimaginable power to answer your cry for help.

Pray

God, I believe you hear my cry for help. I'm listening for your answer.

> "Only when we are depending on God alone are we in a position to see God's help and deliverance."
>
> CATHERINE MARSHALL,
> *Beyond Our Selves*

Strength to Strength

*What joy for those whose strength
comes from the LORD, who have set their
minds on a pilgrimage to Jerusalem.*

PSALM 84:5 NLT

Pause

The longest journey I've taken lasted more than forty hours with long layovers between connecting flights. Both my brain and my body felt depleted by the time I arrived at my destination. Such are the limitations we experience in our mortal selves.

You and I are mere humans, formed from dust. It's no wonder we grow weary on our pilgrimage from earth to heaven. We work outside the home, do daily chores, care for our families, struggle with sickness and injuries, deal with emergencies, and more. It's exhausting, right? But there's hope.

The Lord promises inner strength despite the physical limitations of our mortal, aging bodies. In fact, Psalm 84:5–7 says we will grow consistently stronger until we reach our heavenly home and see God face-to-face.

No self-help program, exercise routine, natural supplement, or magic pill can add strength to strength in us. It's a supernatural gift from the Lord, and we experience it when we keep our minds fixed on him and on all things eternal.

Ponder

For what do you need inner strength today?

Pray

God, thank you for giving me strength upon strength as I travel through this world to heaven.

"You are stronger than you think, because the power of Almighty God is available to you. Your strength is renewed when you trust in Him."

KENDRA TILLMAN,
You Are Stronger Than You Think:
Lessons of Endurance in the Race of Faith

Siri and the Spirit

Your ears shall hear a word behind you, saying,
"This is the way, walk in it," when you turn
to the right or when you turn to the left.

ISAIAH 30:21 ESV

Pause

Driving in unfamiliar territory is scary for directionally challenged me, so I rely on Siri, a virtual assistant provided by Apple's operating system. She tells me which highway exit I should take. She says whether to turn left or right at an upcoming intersection. She even tells me to recalculate, so I can get back on track when I doubt her and go my own way. Only heaven knows where I'd be without her.

As much as I appreciate Siri's voice, I appreciate the Holy Spirit's voice infinitely more. Life's journey can be confusing and scary, especially in unfamiliar territory, but he is with us. When we face major decisions, he guides us. He says when to stop and when to forge ahead with our plans. If we head in the wrong direction, he nudges us to recalculate.

Unlike Siri, the Holy Spirit never makes a mistake or needs to be updated. We can trust every directive he gives us, because he is perfect and has our best interest in mind.

Ponder

For what situation do you desire to hear the Spirit's voice?

Pray

God, open my ears to hear your whispers telling me what to do and where to go.

"Having your spiritual radar up in constant anticipation of His presence—even in the midst of the joyful chaos and regular rhythms of your everyday living—is paramount in hearing God, because sometimes the place and manner you find Him is the least spectacular you'd expect."

PRISCILLA SHIRER,
Gideon: Your Weakness, God's Strength

Yahweh

God replied to Moses, "I AM WHO I AM.
Say this to the people of Israel:
I AM has sent me to you."

EXODUS 3:14 NLT

Pause

God first introduced himself using the name "Yahweh" when speaking to Moses from the burning bush. "Yahweh"—"I am who I am"—implied God's immediate and constant presence. He forever was, forever is, and forever will be. It also declared him as self-existent, self-sustaining, and sovereign over all things. It established him as far superior to the Egyptians' idols familiar to Moses because of his upbringing in Pharaoh's palace.

The idols that the Egyptians worshiped were lifeless, needing human hands to create and sustain them. Each of them supposedly held dominion over a specific aspect of life, but none reigned supreme over everything.

Using a name that set him far above all lesser gods, God showed up in Moses's crisis-of-belief moment. Yahweh guaranteed his presence and power to help Moses, something that the idols could not do.

Modern-day idols woo us to worship them, but they can't begin to measure up to Yahweh. His name says it all, and he is faithful to those who trust in it.

Ponder

Identify a modern-day false god in which you might be tempted to trust when facing challenges.

Pray

God, keep me from relying on anything other than you—Yahweh, the great I AM.

> "Yahweh is the creator of all that there is. He is the most real thing, the only eternal thing. Our hearts will stop beating, our eyes will close, the mountains may someday crumble, the trees will wither away, but Yahweh will always be."
>
> CONNILYN COSSETTE, *Counted with the Stars*

Choices, Choices

Dear brothers and sisters,
when troubles of any kind come your way,
consider it an opportunity for great joy.
For you know that when your faith is tested,
your endurance has a chance to grow.

JAMES 1:2–3 NLT

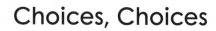

Pause

The pandemic unleashed more than a virus. It infected people with fear, suspicion, and anger. Division struck in so many places—families, churches, workplaces, and governments.

Pandemic-induced tension struck a relationship dear to me. I asked God to bring a resolution, but the divide widened and my heartache grew. One afternoon I experienced a spiritual aha moment: I'd considered the relationship rift a terrible thing. Period. That perspective made everything about it painful. Aligning my thoughts with truth made a healing shift.

When I looked for reasons to be joyful about my situation, I found that God was using it to deepen my prayer life. He was teaching me to extend grace to others who didn't share my opinion. He was showing me how to love others unconditionally.

Viewing this trouble only as a destructive force left me feeling hurt and angry, but choosing to view it as an opportunity for joy helped me appreciate God's behind-the-scenes work.

Ponder

What current concern can you consider an opportunity for joy?

Pray

God, thank you for the opportunities you've entrusted to me at this time. I choose to see them as good.

> "Everything can be taken from a man but one thing: the last of human freedoms—to choose one's attitude in any given set of circumstances, to choose one's own way."
>
> VIKTOR E. FRANKL, *Man's Search for Meaning*

Because You Prayed

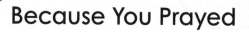

Confess your sins to each other and pray for each other so that you may be healed. The prayer of a righteous person is powerful and effective.

JAMES 5:16

Pause

King Sennacherib of Assyria sent a letter to King Hezekiah warning of an impending attack. He bragged that the gods of other nations had been helpless before his army, and Hezekiah should expect the same outcome.

Hezekiah prayed about the letter's content, and God reassured him that Sennacherib was wrong. God told him that victory would come "because you have prayed to me concerning Sennacherib king of Assyria" (Isaiah 37:21). Then God took action and came to Hezekiah's rescue.

When we encounter battles, we often default to thinking that all we can do is pray. We consider prayer a last resort rather than our first response. In reality, it's a powerful weapon. It's God's invitation to participate in bringing his eternal purposes to pass.

What concerns you today? Lay those concerns before the Lord like Hezekiah laid the letter before God; and with an attitude of surrender and trust, talk to God about those concerns. He will act on them because you pray.

Ponder

What concerns are on your mind today?

Pray

God, I lay my concerns before you and trust you to help me face them with courage and victory.

"Our prayers may be awkward. Our attempts may be feeble. But since the power of prayer is in the one who hears it and not in the one who says it, our prayers do make a difference"

MAX LUCADO, *Grace for the Moment: Inspirational Thoughts for Each Day of the Year* (volume 1)

Wonder

*When I look at the night sky and see the work
of your fingers—the moon and the stars
you set in place—what are mere mortals
that you should think about them, human beings
that you should care for them?*

PSALM 8:3–4 NLT

Pause

Children are born with a sense of wonder, and the shepherd boy David was no exception. Lying on his back and gazing at the star-studded canopy overhead filled him with awe about God's might and majesty and about God's care for him—a mere mortal.

God created me and you with a sense of wonder, too, but it often fades over time. Busyness consumes us, and we buzz past beauty without a second glance. We might fall into the same behavior in our spiritual life. Distracted by demands on our time and attention, we rush into worship that's devoid of the wonder and awe God deserves because of who he is.

Worship minus wonder becomes empty religious tradition; worship with wonder becomes joy-filled friendship with God. That's what he desires for us—a relationship with him rooted in the truth of who he is and overflowing with joy and hope in every situation.

Ponder

What aspect of God's character fills you with wonder and awe?

Pray

God, you are more than amazing, and I am more than blessed because you love me.

> "We don't need a convenient, compact God. We need the One who causes us to fall upon our knees, who leaves us speechless, who makes our eyes shine with His fire and causes us to depart as changed persons. And we need that God every moment of every day."
>
> DAVID JEREMIAH, *My Heart's Desire: Living Every Moment in the Wonder of Worship*

Are We Almost There?

We can rejoice, too, when we run into problems and trials, for we know that they help us develop endurance. And endurance develops strength of character, and character strengthens our confident hope of salvation.

ROMANS 5:3-4 NLT

Pause

Our kids were elementary-school aged when Sailor-Man and I decided to pair his week-long business conference in San Diego with a family vacation. We would drive 1200 miles to make this happen. Before we left town, we made a quick stop at the bank. That's when we heard a child's voice from the backseat: "Are we almost there?"

My child's question describes the way I feel when experiencing an extended challenge. My human nature doesn't like to linger long in a hard place. It wants God to accomplish his purpose pronto. It wants him to hurry up, solve the problem, and end the pain. But he doesn't usually work that way.

God knows the results he wants to achieve in and through our lives through challenges. He also knows that he cannot rush the process. Remembering that he is wise and good and works from an eternal timeline helps us learn patience when our journey feels long.

Ponder

What helpful question might you ask God when your journey feels long?

Pray

God, I don't like lingering in this place, but I will rejoice in the opportunity to develop endurance and hope.

> "When God wants to make a mushroom, he does it overnight, but when he wants to make a giant oak, he takes a hundred years. Great souls are grown through struggles and storms and seasons of suffering. Be patient with the process."
>
> RICK WARREN, *The Purpose Driven Life: What on Earth Am I Here For?*

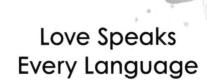

Love Speaks
Every Language

*Three things will last forever—faith, hope, and
love—and the greatest of these is love.*

1 CORINTHIANS 13:13 NLT

Pause

Sailor-Man sat in the aisle seat, I sat in the middle, and an elderly Egyptian woman sat by the window. She visited on her phone until the flight attendant told her to put it away and buckle her seatbelt.

The woman wrestled with the belt to make it fit but without success. Seeing her frustration, I offered my assistance. She spoke no English and I spoke no Arabic, so our combined efforts proved comical, and we shared a good laugh. Then she reached into her bag and retrieved a container filled with homemade treats. She offered me one and then another. I accepted and expressed appreciation, and she smiled. We spent the hour-long flight by looking at each other's family pictures on our phones and ended it with a selfie to celebrate our encounter.

We came from different cultures. She wore different clothes, ate different food, and worshiped a different god than mine. Despite all this, our hearts connected because love speaks every language.

More and more, our journey intersects with people different from ourselves. Let's speak the language of love. Let's build bridges, not walls.

Ponder

Identify someone different from yourself. How can you demonstrate love to that person?

Pray

God, speak your love through me in word and deed.

"One of God's main purposes for your life
is to fill you with so much of His love
that it overflows onto others."

STORMIE OMARTIAN,
The Power of a Praying® Parent

Good News, Great Joy

They were terrified, but the angel reassured them. "Don't be afraid!" he said. "I bring you good news that will bring great joy to all people."

LUKE 2:9–10 NLT

Pause

When the angel announced Jesus' arrival on the night he was born, his message conveyed several truths that God knew humans needed to hear through the ages. First, the angel told the shepherds not to be afraid. Maybe he meant to calm their fears at his appearance, but perhaps he also meant that mankind needn't live in fear because Immanuel—"God with us"—has come. We are not alone.

Second, the angel said he brought good news. Those living under the tyranny of Roman rule must have thought, *Good news? Finally!* I appreciate their feelings. We're barraged by bad news every day. Good news feeds the soul.

Third, the angel promised this news would bring great joy. He didn't say it *might* bring a *little bit* of joy. He meant bucketfuls of joy filled to overflowing.

Finally, he said his message was for all people. No discrimination on any level. And by implication, there's no expiration date.

The angel's message was more than a birth announcement. It was a message infused with hope and was meant to change our lives every day of the year.

Ponder

What part of the angel's message do you appreciate most? Why?

Pray

God, thank you for sending Jesus, hope personified.

"The birth of Jesus made possible not just a new way of understanding life but a new way of living it."

FREDERICK BUECHNER,
The Faces of Jesus: A Life Story

Burden Bearer

Jesus said, "Come to me, all of you who
are weary and carry heavy burdens,
and I will give you rest. For my yoke is easy to bear,
and the burden I give you is light."

MATTHEW 11:28, 30 NLT

Pause

Traveling alone to a women's retreat, I boarded the plane and hoisted my suitcase into the overhead bin. That's when a searing pain ripped through my left shoulder.

The injury crippled me for months. Unable to lift anything above my head, I asked God to send help every time I had to fly alone. He answered. Without fail, either the gate attendant offered to check my bag for free, or a gentleman in a seat near mine stood and stowed my suitcase in the overhead bin.

We can sustain injuries of another sort when we carry heavy emotional burdens. Jesus knows our limitations, so he offers to lift such burdens from our shoulders. If we insist on taking responsibility for them, their weight will eventually exhaust us and rob us of joy and peace. That's not the way he wants us to live.

"Let me help you," says Jesus. Gratefully accept his offer, and give him your burdens.

Ponder

What weight are you carrying today?

Pray

God, thank you for offering to carry my burdens. Here they are—I give them to you with gratitude.

> "Usually we think that the human will must be strengthened, but paradoxically you become stronger only when you become weaker. When you surrender your will to God, you finally discover the resources to do what God requires."
>
> ERWIN W. LUTZER, *Winning the Inner War: How to Say No to a Stubborn Habit*

God's Power Displayed

*He gives power to the faint, and to him
who has no might he increases strength.*

ISAIAH 40:29 ESV

Pause

Kathy sat at her mother's bedside and listened to the elderly woman's illogical chatter. A decade-long descent into Alzheimer's had taken its toll, and nothing her mother said made sense—until Kathy asked her to talk about Jesus.

In Kathy's words, her mother "closed her eyes and peace settled over her face. Her voice filled with awe and her words made so much sense. 'He is so good. He is so powerful. He helps me. He is so wonderful.'" She continued to describe Jesus for several minutes before reverting to meaningless conversation.

Kathy had frequently asked God to give her mom an awareness of his presence. Those bittersweet moments provided her the joy of seeing his answer. They also gave her the opportunity to see God's power displayed.

Our human nature tends to view weakness as a hardship, a fault, or even something shameful. No doubt, living in a weakened state or watching a loved one struggle in such a state presents challenges. But when we're surrendered to Jesus, frailty needn't be feared. It becomes the backdrop against which God's strength and might are seen. It provides a stage on which his power working in us performs best.

Ponder

How have you seen God's power at work in weakness?

Pray

God, make my life your stage where others can see your power demonstrated.

> "Our human frailty serves to magnify the glorious power of God. When we are not able to stand on our own, God's grace and strength are displayed. Our weakness is an opportunity for God to demonstrate what only He can do."
>
> KATHY HOWARD, author of *Heirloom: Living and Leaving a Legacy of Faith.*

Beyond Imagination

*Now to him who is able to do immeasurably more
than all we ask or imagine, according to his power
that is at work within us, to him be glory in the
church and in Christ Jesus throughout all
generations, for ever and ever! Amen.*

EPHESIANS 3:20-21

Pause

Two relatives volunteered their services at our missionary staff conference in Slovakia. They'd never traveled overseas, so we decided to meet in London's Heathrow Airport and complete the journey together.

Heavy fog caused havoc for hundreds of incoming flights that day, theirs and mine included, and I worried about how the volunteers were faring. "God, help me find them," I prayed.

Two hours later, I joined the masses clearing Passport Control. I headed to a line on my right, but a security guard redirected me to the left. And guess who was standing at the end of that line?

The against-all-odds meeting rendered us speechless at God's care for us. It opened my eyes to God's ability to abundantly exceed anything we can ask or imagine, and it challenged me to pray big and expect even bigger answers.

Ponder

For what would you like God to do immeasurably more than you can imagine?

Pray

God, please answer my prayers in a way beyond imagination and bring glory to your name.

> "There is no promise too hard for God to fulfill.
> No prayer is too big for him to answer!"
>
> CHRISTINE CAINE

God's Consolations

When I said, "My foot is slipping,"
your unfailing love, LORD, supported me.
When anxiety was great within me,
your consolation brought me joy.

PSALM 94:18–19

Pause

The sun's scorching heat baked the bus in which Sailor-Man and I rode. With three hours behind us and three still before us, I wondered whether I'd survive the ride. The vehicle had no air-conditioning, and the windows opened only a crack. Sweat soaked my face, neck, and back. Worse, we had no drinking water. We'd boarded the bus, assuming we could buy bottled water at a stop. Unfortunately, the bus stopped only once to allow passengers to stretch and smoke by the roadside.

I rested my forehead on the rail in front of us and prayed, "I can't do this anymore, God. Help!" He responded by bringing a favorite worship song to mind. He followed the song with Scripture verses that recalled his faithfulness. Then he prompted me to count my blessings. He supported and consoled me, and he brought me joy.

The temperature didn't change, but my attitude did. I stopped worrying about not surviving the ride and began looking forward to soon seeing dear friends in our destination city.

Ponder

How does the Lord support you when you feel like you're slipping?

Pray

God, let's trade. I'll give you my worries in exchange for your consolation and joy.

> "When trust in God grows, joy has the freedom to grow as well. We cannot have joy and worry at the same time.... 'When you're worrying, you're not trusting. And when you're trusting, you're not worrying.'"
>
> KAY WARREN,
> *Choose Joy: Because Happiness Isn't Enough*

Today's a Gift

Let those who dwell in the dust
wake up and shout for joy.

ISAIAH 26:19

Pause

Janet and her four kids piled into their car. She'd taught high school English all week and anticipated spending the weekend at her parents' home three hours away. She just wanted to get there. The kids? Not so much.

One after another, the older three asked to stop, but Janet refused. Then the fourth asked to stop at a dairy farm that could be seen at an approaching intersection.

Before Janet could answer, she felt compelled to hit the brakes. A moment later, a car raced through the intersection, missing her car by two feet. Shaking, she parked on the shoulder by the dairy farm and rolled down her window. After their brush with death, that dairy air smelled pretty good.

Sometimes we get so busy that we forget to look for evidences of God's goodness. We focus more on achieving goals than loving people, and we miss the blessings prepared for us. God intends better for us.

Every day is a gift. Thank the Giver, and ask him how he wants you to use the day. His answer will always honor his ways, and partnering with him will bring joy.

Ponder

If it were possible, what's one thing you would change about your routine day, and why?

Pray

God, teach me to appreciate the gift of today and to use it for your intended purpose.

> "Life always smells good
> when truly appreciated."
>
> JANET HOLM MCHENRY, author of *PrayerWalk: Becoming a Woman of Prayer, Strength, and Discipline*

The Key to Hope

*Finally, brothers and sisters, whatever is true,
whatever is noble, whatever is right, whatever is
pure, whatever is lovely, whatever is admirable—
if anything is excellent or praiseworthy—
think about such things.*

PHILIPPIANS 4:8

Pause

Two sisters spoke with me about a family crisis they faced.
First one and then the other offered her perspective. The
first concluded that all hope was gone. The individual
about whom they were concerned would never change,
and circumstances were beyond repair. Why expect
anything better when disappointment was almost certain?
She reminded me of Eeyore, the downcast donkey of
Winnie the Pooh fame.

The second sister felt that the individual involved could
and would change. She spoke of the power of persistent
prayer, of trusting God to fulfill his promises, and of God's
power to do the seemingly impossible.

We're all created with unique personalities that help shape our perspective toward challenges. At the same time, we're all given a choice that can override a negative bent. The thoughts we habitually think are the determining factor. Focusing on what-ifs and impossibilities reinforces the negative. But focusing on truth reinforces hope.

Choose well, my friend. Choose hope.

Ponder

Consider your thought patterns. What's your natural bent?

Pray

God, teach me to use the key you've provided to open the door to hope.

> "We can choose to gather to our hearts the thorns of disappointment, failure, loneliness, and dismay in our present situation. Or we can gather the flowers of God's grace, boundless love, abiding presence, and unmatched joy. I choose to gather the flowers."
>
> BARBARA JOHNSON,
> *Fresh Elastic for Stretched Out Moms*

Worship Despite Disappointment

Then David got up from the ground, washed himself, put on lotions, and changed his clothes. He went to the Tabernacle and worshiped the LORD.

2 SAMUEL 12:20 NLT

Pause

When his infant son became ill, King David fasted and prayed for the baby's health to be restored. God answered his prayers with a no. The Bible doesn't explicitly say so, but we might assume David felt disappointed, even heartbroken, with the outcome. Nevertheless, he rose from the prostrate position he'd held for a week, cleaned himself, and went to the Tabernacle to worship God.

Disappointment is defined by one dictionary as "sadness or displeasure caused by the nonfulfillment of one's hopes or expectations." The pandemic dumped disappointments galore without discretion. No one was immune, and everyone had to decide how to deal with them. Many folks responded either with resignation or by acting out their frustration. But some responded with worship, just like King David did.

God desires our worship in the midst of our disappointments. It demonstrates humility—the attitude that acknowledges him as the final authority over our lives. It tells the Lord that we choose to trust his wisdom and his ways, even when we don't understand, and it frees him to accomplish good purposes in us.

Ponder

What does worshiping the Lord in the midst of disappointment look like for you?

Pray

God, fill my heart with worship when unmet expectations bring sadness or displeasure.

> "The long series of disappointments you accumulate in a lifetime can stop you from moving forward into all the goodness God has planned for you—and that means they'll be stopping not only you, but also all those God has destined you to reach along your life journey."
>
> CHRISTINE CAINE,
> *Undaunted: Daring to Do What God Calls You to Do*

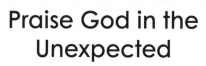

Praise God in the Unexpected

I will praise the name of God with a song;
I will magnify him with thanksgiving.

PSALM 69:30 ESV

Pause

Linda was driving down the interstate and singing along with "Holy Is the Lamb" when a monster storm cloud suddenly swallowed her vehicle. The pelting rain turned into ice and became like a fire hose of slush sprayed the windshield, and the air pressure changed inside the car. An oil tanker driving beside her vanished momentarily, reappeared for several seconds, and then disappeared again into a second wall of fury before both vehicles popped back into the sunshine. Throughout the craziness, she kept singing alleluias about the Lord Almighty's reign.

Linda later learned that she'd survived a brush with a killer tornado that flattened 78 homes. She likens her experience to being hit by the unexpected on our life's journey. All is well one minute, but everything changes in the next.

As Linda discovered, praise is our best defense when the unexpected catches us off guard. Darkness descends and wind screams around us, but remembering—and declaring—that God rules over every detail of our lives fills us with calm. Praising him for his presence and sovereignty guards our hearts from panic and fills us with courage and peace.

Ponder

What worship song is especially meaningful to you, and why?

Pray

God, put a song of praise to you in my heart when the storm winds blow.

> "God holds our hand in the storm. He'll not only help us get through it, but he will help us sing songs of worship above the howling winds."
>
> LINDA EVANS SHEPHERD, author of *Praying Through Every Emotion: Experiencing God's Peace No Matter What*

Greater Joy

You [LORD] have given me greater joy than those who have abundant harvests of grain and new wine.

PSALM 4:7 NLT

Pause

Different things bring different levels of joy to different people. Here's an incomplete list of my joy-starters: prayer walking, rising early for quiet time with Jesus, playing with my grandchildren, baking cinnamon buns, and hosting come-and-go coffee times for our neighbors. No doubt you have a list of your own.

The psalmist indicated that some folks in his circle found joy in prosperity. Perhaps an abundant harvest enabled them to pay their debts, give generously to people less fortunate, or celebrate God's goodness with friends and family. Certainly these things could bring joy to one's heart, but the psalmist said he found even greater joy in the Lord.

Reasons for finding joy in the Lord are many: He is present in our circumstances. He shelters us under his wing and guards us with his promises (Psalm 91:4). He leads and provides (Psalm 23). He forgives our sin and sets us free from fear and shame (1 John 1:9; Psalm 34:4–5).

For sure, this is an incomplete list. After all, knowing and trusting God opens up all sorts of possibilities for joy.

Ponder

Name something about God that brings you great joy.

Pray

God, you bring me greater joy than anything on my joy-starter list.

> "We will never be happy until we make *God* the source of our fulfillment and the answer to our longings. He is the *only* one who should have power over our souls."
>
> STORMIE OMARTIAN,
> *The Power of a Praying® Woman*

The Power of Song

I will sing to the LORD as long as I live.
I will praise my God to my last breath!

PSALM 104:33 NLT

Pause

My two-year-old granddaughter, Lexi, always asks me to sing at bedtime. One of our favorites is "Jesus Loves Me."

> Jesus loves me—this I know,
> For the Bible tells me so.
> Little ones to him belong;
> They are weak, but he is strong.
> Yes, Jesus loves me! Yes, Jesus loves me!
> Yes, Jesus loves me! The Bible tells me so.

I learned this song as a little girl, and the lyrics remain with me six decades later. The truth of the lyrics has withstood the test of time, and the song has carried me across many miles—both literally and figuratively. It strengthens me when the road feels long and steep. It encourages me when darkness hides my way and I feel afraid.

Worship songs are powerful, like mighty weapons to help us conquer our enemies on our journey. No matter how many miles we've traveled or where we are on the map, they serve to remind us of truth. In this case, it's basic but life-changing. Simple but profound.

Jesus loves us. We belong to him. The Bible tells us so.

Ponder

Sing or speak aloud the lyrics to "Jesus Loves Me" as written in today's meditation.

Pray

God, deepen my understanding of your love until my heart bursts into songs of praise.

> "Part of the power of song is that it is a beautiful expression of devotion.... Singing releases the pent-up joy and thanksgiving we feel because of God's grace and goodness."
>
> JACK HAYFORD, *The Heart of Praise: Worship after God's Own Heart*

Trust

You love him even though you have never seen him.
Though you do not see him now, you trust him;
and you rejoice with a glorious, inexpressible joy.

1 PETER 1:8 NLT

Pause

Joy is—or rather, should be—a hallmark of every person who professes to follow Jesus. We have every reason to face challenges with a settled assurance that all will be well because God's promises surround us, his presence fills us, and his power equips us.

Joy evaporates when we forget these truths. We fall into wrong thinking about God's intent toward us, his love for us, and his desire to spend eternity with us. Joy dissipates when we further forget to apply a five-letter word tucked in the middle of today's verse. That word is *trust*.

Trusting God doesn't come easily when we hold incorrect beliefs about him. Doubting his love, for instance, leads us to question his care for us. *Will he really provide for me? Will he really forgive me again?* Uncertainty and fear override joy.

Everything changes when we trust the Lord. We give him our concerns and let him take control. Our load moves from our shoulders to his, and joy returns.

Ponder

With what concerns can you easily trust God? What's more difficult to give him?

Pray

God, you are faithful, but my trust is fickle. Deepen my trust and restore my joy.

"Faith at its heart is about trust. It's one thing to believe in God; it's quite something else to trust him with our lives. We all want deeper relationships built on trust."

RICK PERRY

Community

Share each other's burdens,
and in this way obey the law of Christ.

GALATIANS 6:2 NLT

Pause

I travel alone frequently for ministry commitments and it's doable, but I prefer traveling with a companion. Sailor-Man, of course, usually fills that role.

When driving by car, we take turns behind the wheel, so the other can work or rest. When the road feels long and we feel weary, the passenger helps keep the driver alert.

In airports, we take turns sitting with our luggage, freeing the other to take a walk. I keep the boarding passes, and he stows our suitcases in the overhead compartments aboard the plane. We look out for the other's well-being and we share responsibilities. It works well for both of us.

God placed humans in community for a reason: we need one another. Isolation isn't healthy. The pandemic revealed this is true. Friends provide companionship in good times and bad. They spur us on when the road feels long, and they help carry our load when we're weak.

God never meant for us to take life's journey alone, so find a friend, and be a friend. In community is where we flourish best.

Ponder

What qualities do you value most in a friendship?

Pray

God, help me be a friend on whom others can rely through their thick or thin.

> "Belonging to a caring community that is linked to God gives us people to share both our joys and sorrows. Our joys are doubled and our sorrows are halved."
>
> MAX ANDERS, *What You Need to Know about the Church in Twelve Lessons*

Always Available

*I will call to you whenever I'm in trouble,
and you will answer me.*

PSALM 86:7 NLT

Pause

Sailor-Man and I occasionally touch base with family back home in North America when we travel internationally. Technology has provided various ways to do that, for which I'm grateful. Still, we deal with challenges, things like unreliable connections that drop our conversation mid-call, and coordinating a time to talk that's convenient for both parties, considering the nine- to twelve-hour gap between us.

Aren't you glad that communicating with the Lord doesn't involve such issues? Members of God's family can be grateful that through Jesus Christ's death and resurrection, we have ready access to God through prayer. We can call our heavenly Father any time—day or night—with full assurance that he hears and will answer us.

Imagine your life if time zones restricted access to God and forced you to schedule conversations to avoid catching him at an inconvenient time. Imagine the feelings of disappointment if your intercessory line dropped mid-prayer.

We are beyond blessed that God has provided a way—without technology—to touch base with him wherever we are and whenever we wish and that he hears us and answers us.

Ponder

Tell God how much you love him. Do it now. No worries—you're not interrupting him.

Pray

God, I'm so glad I can call on you, knowing you're there and ready to talk.

> "God waits for you to communicate with Him. You have instant, direct access to God. God loves mankind so much, and in a very special sense His children, that He has made Himself available to you at all times."
>
> WESLEY L. DUEWEL, *Touch the World through Prayer*

The Spirit

When the Father sends the Advocate as
my representative—that is, the Holy Spirit—
he will teach you everything and will remind
you of everything I have told you.

JOHN 14:26 NLT

Pause

Some of British Columbia's coastal islands are provincial marine parks equipped to provide safe anchorage for pleasure craft. When Sailor-Man and I visit these parks, we first set our anchor on the sea bottom. Then, using a floating rope, we tie our vessel to a chain that's embedded in the rocky shoreline behind us. We utilize the park's provision to ensure that our boat won't drift into craft on either side and cause damage or injury.

God has blessed us with his Word to anchor our hearts in truth and hope. He has also provided the Holy Spirit to ensure our well-being during our stay on earth. The Spirit comforts, teaches, and guides us. He prays for us

(Romans 8:26). He produces in us godly character traits, such as love, joy, patience, and peace (Galatians 5:22–23).

As boaters utilize the marine park chains, so you and I must utilize the provision God has made for us. He ensures our well-being, so let's invite his involvement in every part of our lives.

Ponder

How does the Holy Spirit's presence make a difference in your life?

Pray

God, keep me mindful of the Holy Spirit's presence and power in my life.

> "God knows what each one of us is dealing with. He knows our pressures. He knows our conflicts. And He has made a provision for each and every one of them. That provision is Himself in the person of the Holy Spirit, indwelling us and empowering us to *respond rightly*."
>
> KAY ARTHUR, *As Silver Refined: Learning to Embrace Life's Disappointments*

Precious Words

When your words came, I ate them;
they were my joy and my heart's delight,
*for I bear your name, L*ORD *God Almighty.*

JEREMIAH 15:16

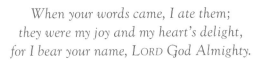

Pause

Spoken and written words bombard us every day. My head spins sometimes because words come at me from so many different directions, especially on social media. Some words there inspire me. Some make me laugh. Others make me shake my head and wonder what their author was thinking when he or she posted them. How different they are from God's holy words!

The prophet Jeremiah wrote that God's words brought joy and delight to his heart. He heard them, savored them, and internalized them. He accepted them as true and good because he knew their Author and trusted his integrity and wisdom.

We live in a society where words come cheap. They're often used to cast doubt, attack, criticize, and influence others to think a desired way. Again, how different they are from God's words written to encourage, guide, comfort, and instruct us toward holy living.

Let's treasure God's words as Jeremiah did. After all, we know the Author. He wrote them from a heart of love and for our good.

Ponder

Recall a time when God's words bore a significant influence on your life.

Pray

God, create in me an insatiable hunger for your words.

> "The truth you store up in silence comes back to you in the storm, and it lifts you away as on a life raft from the fears and disappointments that would otherwise pull you under. When you abide in his word, he abides in you."
>
> CHRISTINE CAINE, *Undaunted: Daring to Do What God Calls You to Do*

The Right Path

This is what the LORD says:
"Stop at the crossroads and look around. Ask for the
old, godly way, and walk in it. Travel its path,
and you will find rest for your souls. But you reply,
"No, that's not the road we want!"

JEREMIAH 6:16 NLT

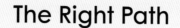

Sailor-Man and I biked through Germany into Austria with another couple. One afternoon, we faced a fork in the road when we rolled into a village where we'd made hotel reservations. A motorcyclist saw us studying a map and stopped to help us. He knew the hotel, so he led us to it.

We were strangers to the area and weary from the day's ride. Following the local was the only logical thing to do, right? Refusing his help or insisting on taking a different road would have been nonsensical.

Our souls crave rest from turmoil. God has given us tried-and-true directions to find that safe place. Our culture offers various routes that might seem appealing, but they will lead us astray. It's in our best interest to follow Jesus and his teachings (John 10:27). He knows better than we do how to find our way. Accepting his help makes sense, right?

Ponder

How has following God's path brought a blessing your way?

Pray

God, grant me the desire to follow you with enthusiasm on the path you know is best.

> "I believe Christians often perceive obedience to God as some test designed just to see if we're really committed to him. But what if it's designed as God's way of giving us what's best for us?"
>
> CRAIG GROESCHEL,
> *Altar Ego: Becoming Who God Says You Are*

Nothing's Impossible

Nothing will be impossible with God.

LUKE 1:37 ESV

Pause

Jesus is the master of turning impossibilities into possibilities. Think about it: his earthly life began with a virgin birth. Impossible? Absolutely. He turned water into wine, healed the lame and the lepers, calmed stormy seas with a single command, and fed thousands with a few loaves and fish. Impossible? Certainly. But not for Jesus.

Miracles marked Jesus' life. They also marked his death: The tomb held his neatly folded grave clothes, but it couldn't hold him (Mark 16:6). Neither could locked rooms stop him from gaining entry (John 20:19).

At some point, our journey leads to a valley called Impossible. Obstacles, like mountains, surround us and tower above us. Their shadows loom and block our vision. We see no pathway, no provision, no answer, no way out.

Moving beyond the impossible seems, well, impossible. But the truth is that this is the place where Jesus does some of his finest work. He asks us to trust him and then, in his perfect time and way, he shows up and does something only he can do.

We needn't fear the valley called Impossible. If God has led us there, he'll surely lead us out. Everything is possible with him.

Ponder

Recall a time when Jesus turned an impossibility into a possibility.

Pray

God, I trust you to lead me from the valley of impossibility to the mountaintop of possibility.

> "In the midst of uncertainty and the paradoxical tension of having to believe God for the impossible, real faith requires actually trusting in *Him*, despite our inability to always understand Him."
>
> KEN WYTSMA, *The Grand Paradox: The Messiness of Life, the Mystery of God, and the Necessity of Faith*

One Thing

The Lord answered her, "Martha, Martha, you are anxious and troubled about many things, but one thing is necessary. Mary has chosen the good portion, which will not be taken away from her."

LUKE 10:41–42 ESV

Pause

Jesus considered sisters Mary and Martha as dear friends. It's no wonder, then, that Martha wanted to bless him when he arrived at their door with disciples in tow. Her desire to serve sent her scurrying about the kitchen and, sadly, drove her stress level sky-high. When she complained that she was working while Mary sat at Jesus' feet, Jesus reminded her to keep the main thing the main thing. That is, time in his presence.

Life's concerns and busyness—and even our desire to serve Jesus—can easily divert us from what matters most. We race down the path of trying to do everything and be everything to everyone. Before long, we're winded physically, emotionally, mentally, and spiritually. And it shows. Peace and joy—gone.

Returning to the one thing that matters most sets our feet on the right track. Prioritizing friendship with Jesus renews us for the tasks at hand and restores the peace and joy our hearts desire.

Ponder

What other things in your life have replaced the main thing?

Pray

God, grant me the desire and ability to pursue one thing above all else.

"A rule I have had for years is to treat the Lord Jesus Christ as a personal friend. He is not a creed, a mere doctrine; but it is He Himself we have."

DWIGHT LYMAN MOODY,
The Gospel Awakening

Seek God's Face

When You said, "Seek My face," my heart
said to You, "I shall seek Your face, LORD."

PSALM 27:8 NASB

Pause

Sailor-Man and I anchored in a cove where nature's beauty beckoned me every morning. I rose early to sit in silence and enjoy my surroundings. The effort rewarded me with sights and sounds I would not have experienced otherwise: fish jumping, seals slapping their tails on the water's surface, birds diving for breakfast and then bobbing up to swallow their catch, and more.

I experienced nature's beauty by spending quiet time in nature. I've discovered the same principle works in the spiritual realm. We experience the Lord's beauty by spending time with him simply for the sake of enjoying his presence.

God beckons us. We might think that today we're too busy or we're under too much stress to make time to sit with no agenda in God's presence, even for a few minutes, but the truth is that time spent with him determines the direction our journey takes and the scope of our ability to cope. Accept his invitation to join him, and he'll reward your effort.

Ponder

What needs to happen so that you can have a few minutes of agenda-free silence in God's presence today?

Pray

God, grant me success as I seek to make time solely with you, and speak to me in that place.

"Worship-based prayer seeks the face of God before the hand of God. God's face is the essence of who He is. God's hand is the blessing of what He does. God's face represents His person and presence. God's hand expresses His provision for needs in our lives. I have learned that if all we ever do is seek God's hand, we may miss His face; but if we seek His face, He will be glad to open His hand and satisfy the deepest desires of our hearts."

JENNIFER KENNEDY DEAN,
Prayer Fatigue: Ten Ways to Revive Your Prayer Life

Joy for Now

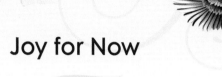

You make known to me the path of life;
in your presence there is fullness of joy;
at your right hand are pleasures forevermore.

PSALM 16:11 ESV

Pause

When we read Psalm 16:11, we might assume the writer was referring to the end of our earthly journey—when we reach heaven. For sure we'll enjoy Jesus' presence and the pleasures he has prepared for us when that time comes, but there's more to the verse than that.

The psalmist's words also refer to the here and now, because God dwells with us. He walks with us through both the mundane times and the moments that leave us breathless. He's with us whether we're alone or in the middle of a crowd. When we wake and when we sleep, he's there.

In his presence we experience pleasures here on this earth: A baby's giggle. A moonlit night. A gentle snowfall.

The smell of bacon sizzling over a campfire. The sight of frolicking colts in spring. Unexpected answers to prayer.

Yes, our journey will one day lead to heaven where we'll meet Jesus face-to-face, and our joy will surpass anything imaginable. But until then, he's given us everything we need to enjoy the life he's given us here and now.

Ponder

What brings you joy in the here and now?

Pray

God, I look forward to unimaginable joy in heaven, but I'm grateful for the joy you supply today.

> "Joy means the perfect fulfilment of that for which I was created and regenerated, not the successful doing of a thing."
>
> OSWALD CHAMBERS,
> *My Utmost for His Highest*

Abide

*If you keep my commandments, you will abide
in my love, just as I have kept my Father's
commandments and abide in his love.
These things I have spoken to you, that my joy
may be in you, and that your joy may be full.*

JOHN 15:10–11 ESV

Pause

Jesus and joy go hand in hand, and he wants the same for us. That's why he spent time talking about joy with his disciples only a few hours before his arrest. It was like he was saying, "Hey, fellows, this is ultra-important. Listen up before I'm gone!"

The key to joy, said Jesus, is found in abiding in his love and obeying his commands. *Abiding with Jesus* means staying in and cultivating a close relationship with him. We do this by spending time in his Word and talking with him. As our love for him grows deeper, our desire to honor him through obedience to his commands also grows.

Jesus practiced what he preached. He stayed in close relationship with God the Father, surrendered to his will, and overflowed with joy—the same joy that he promises to pour into us when we abide and obey.

Joy is accessible to everyone who wants it. We only have to walk hand in hand with Jesus.

Ponder

What's one action you can take to abide in Jesus' love today?

Pray

God, help me follow Jesus' example. As he walked with you, so I want to walk with him.

> "Abiding in Jesus isn't fixing our attention on Christ, but it is being one with Him ... A man is abiding just as much when he is sleeping for Jesus as when he is awake and working for Jesus. Oh, it is a very sweet thing to have one's mind just resting there."
>
> J. HUDSON TAYLOR,
> author of *China's Spiritual Need and Claims*

Meet Grace

Grace is a devotional blogger, member of the First 5 writing team (Proverbs 31 Ministries), co-host of the "Your Daily Bible Verse" podcast, and popular speaker at women's retreats and conferences internationally.

Her passion is to connect the dots between faith and real life by helping her audiences learn to love, understand, and apply God's Word for life transformation. Besides writing and speaking, she's a career global worker and enjoys training others for short-term and career missions. She and her husband live on a sailboat near Vancouver, British Columbia.

Be sure to read the other devotionals in this series: *Finding Hope in Crisis: Devotions for Calm in Chaos* and *Keeping Hope Alive: Devotions for Strength in the Storm*. Available wherever Christian books are sold.

www.gracefox.com
grace@gracefox.com
www.fb.com/gracefox.author
www.instagram.com/graceloewenfox/

More from Grace Fox

A diagnosis. Death of a loved one. A layoff. A broken relationship. Life changes in a nanosecond when storms sweep in, often without warning. They leave our knuckles white and our hearts broken. With minds barely able to think clearly, we often set our Bible aside. In reality, that's when we need its comfort and strength most. These devotionals are written for those in crisis, for those longing for hope but lacking the ability to focus on a lengthy Scripture passage. These minute-sized devotions offer respite to readers caught in the storms of life.

FINDING HOPE IN CRISIS
Devotions to Calm the Chaos

ISBN: 978-1-62862-992-7

KEEPING HOPE ALIVE
Devotions for Strength in the Storm

ISBN: 978-1-64938-051-7

www.hendricksonrose.com